The Mighty Hand

The Mighty Hand

Wrongfully Convicted, Rightfully Freed

Anthony Faison

TATE PUBLISHING
AND ENTERPRISES, LLC

Published by Tate Publishing & Enterprises, LLC
127 E. Trade Center Terrace | Mustang, Oklahoma 73064 USA
1.888.361.9473 | www.tatepublishing.com

Tate Publishing is committed to excellence in the publishing industry. The company reflects the philosophy established by the founders, based on Psalm 68:11,
"The Lord gave the word and great was the company of those who published it."

Book design copyright © 2013 by Tate Publishing, LLC. All rights reserved.
Cover design by Antoine Williams
Interior design by Jomar Ouano

Published in the United States of America

ISBN: 978-1-62854-358-2
1. Biography & Autobiography / Personal Memoirs
2. True Crime / Murder / General
13.07.09

𝔄cknowledgements

Special thanks to all community-based organizations that believed and support men and women in prisons throughout the world. It is from your understanding and kindness that men like me are free today.

To: Lilah

From: Anthony Faison

It was a pleasure seeing you again. 2014

Special thanks to:

Michael S. Race, Ronald L. Kuby, Daniel M. Perez, Sarah Wallace, Robert Crudup, my family whom I love deeply, and Evelyn, my sister.

Some stories have a tendency to be drawn out and dull, to linger on the nondescript things as if they really mattered. I, on the other hand, as I've sat in front of my computer for the past two years, refuse to let you sit in that big chair and read something that will make you toss this book in the corner. My story is as real as the sun that sets every morning and the moon that illuminates the night.

My name is Anthony Faison, and I was wrongfully convicted in the State of New York in the year of 1987. I subsequently spent the next fourteen years in prison. Those painful years molded me into the person that I am today. Those lost years from my life shaped my thought pattern and instilled in me a great sense of patience and understanding concerning my life and all things around me. Please do not take this last sentence as if prison made me a better person—it did not. I do not want to plant that concept in your mind. Prison definition of *being* in the dictionary, you will see my point.

What I want to say is something that any man might say when confronted with an ordeal as powerful as the story I'm about to reveal to you. *Lord, help me.*

𝔄 𝔚𝔞𝔯𝔪 𝔥𝔬𝔪𝔢

(Birth-1987)

Growing up in a two-parent home was special to me as a child. I went to school with classmates who did not have a mother and a father living at home. When I would mention that both my parents lived with me, I felt resentment that I could not understand then. During that time, the average household raising children did not have both parents; it was primarily the mother, and she did so with great love and affection. However, there were parents during that time who were more conscientious of the emotional and psychological needs for their children's welfare than their own selfish needs and wants; my parents fit that mark and I loved them both. I didn't know it at the time, but their act of love and respect for one another nurtured me as to how I would present myself as I would one day raise children of my own.

My father, Fred, worked hard during those early years. I watched him as any little boy would watch their father. I was innocent. I wanted to see what I would be like, watching and understanding him. I was envisioning, through him, how I would grow up and become a man. He was a strong man who worked ten-hour shifts six days a week to provide for his family. He was a man of average build and strong shoulders. Smooth caramel skin, curly hair, a warm smile, and strong Native American features.

I remember how my mother would greet him at the door. No matter how tired she might've been during the day, she always perked up nearing the time of my father's arrival. She would hug him while leading him in to the living room to help him remove his work clothes and shoes. Afterward, she would massage his neck as he settled into his favorite chair in front of the television. We were all aware that my father's chair was the king's chair.

Their affection for each other made me feel warm inside. They loved each other, and they weren't uncomfortable to display it. I had to be about eleven at the time. It's funny now as I tell this story how I can see those images of my parents as it happened yesterday. My sister and I used to laugh at their emotional connection and the love they had for one another; it was all giggles to us. What did we know? We were young.

I was the middle child. My older brother, Jerome (who we call Tis), and my twin sister, Evelyn, all respected and enjoyed one another's company in the sense that we were family. My mother, Sadie, came from the South as my father had a firm hand when it came to disciplining us. I had many aunts on my mother's side who would call us for birthdays and graduations. My mother believed in a family that ate together, so every evening at six o'clock, we all had to be at the dinner table. There were times when I did not want to eat at six o'clock. I wanted to be with my friends during a Saturday or Sunday evening, but that was what I wanted and what I wanted at that age really didn't matter to my parents. They would send my older brother Tis out to find me. That was a confrontation in itself. Older brothers have a tendency to be the father in some instances. Tis was no different whenever he came looking for me. He was about twelve pounds heavier than I was, and he carried himself with an airy, prideful persona.

We were living in Brooklyn, near Marcy Projects, at this time and during those late 1970s and early 1980s, Brooklyn, New York, was a hellfire in itself. These were maddening times filled with questionable characters running the streets that cared about no one or any laws. If something were to catch the eye of these questionable men and women, you better believe they would get it regardless of who was watching. Hustlers, drug dealers, gang bangers, all lost within the evolution of destruction.

I was thirteen at the time, and it was a Saturday evening. It was the summer time in August. I had become engrossed in the crowd I was running with since that morning when I came outside to play, a few of my childhood friends and a few of the neighborhood tomboy girls. Shawna, in particular, although a tomboy who played tough with us boys, was a girl in every way of the word. She had the cutest, smallest red lips that made me blush whenever she'd get close to me. And mind you, her breasts, at fourteen, were like a grown woman's. That girl was beautiful! Anyway, we were in the back of Marcy Project playing the game hot peas and butter. If you come out the ghetto, you know about that game. Well, at that moment, Carlton, a boy who I went to school with, had hidden the belt and was doing the countdown. "You're getting hot. You're on fire." This remark is made when the person searching for the belt is so near to it that they are about to grab it from the hiding location. Once the belt was located, the person would set out to use it on the nearest person.

Shawna, at the time, was the searcher for the belt. She and I were standing beside a worn, weather-beaten tan sofa that someone had used until they could not use it anymore and then threw it in the garbage. I was to the right of her and was looking under and sticking my hand down the seat cushion for the belt. I wanted to find that belt to impress Shawna. She did not pay me any attention as she searched the other end of the sofa. I would glance at her from time to time as I heard Carlton continue to give a description of how cold or hot we were to retrieving the belt. I surreptitiously glanced to the back of the sofa when I saw an old, ragged, blue cloth lying near the leg of the sofa. Under the blue cloth, I saw the glistening sight of a belt buckle. I sighed. I did not want to whip Shawna with the belt. She was too beautiful for me to be hitting her. My infatuation with her was painful at times as I glanced at her a second time. I had to come up with a plan.

Now you might think that that was some real soft, weak, girly thing to do, but man, I was thirteen and my nose was wide open and as wide as the Brooklyn Bridge when it came to Shawna. Damn! That girl was fine! So I maneuvered her to my current position by telling her to let me get to her side so I could rip the bottom of the sofa to see if the belt was there. She resisted for a brief moment. She was suspicious; she stared at me with her light-brown eyes that made my heart flutter. We held eye contact for a full minute, and then she relented. With our positions switched, we continued to search. I heard Carlton run over and begin the countdown.

"You're hot! You're getting hotter! You're on fire!"

That's when I saw Shawna bend down and grab the belt. I and all the other kids playing the game took to running in different directions as Shawna gave chase to anyone she could hit. She might've been top heavy, but she could move as she swung that belt.

Sure, I could've taken the belt and whipped Shawna with it, but for what? I liked her. As I was making a turn around the corner in hopes she would follow me so I could drop my game down on her by telling her that I liked her. Instead, I felt someone pull on the back of my shirt. The strength of the person nearly lifted me off my feet. Man, I thought. Shawna is strong. As I turned around with a big smile on my face, ready to explore the possibilities of me and her becoming friends, I was greeted with the sight of my brother Tis—damn.

Tis always had a serious expression—don't mess with me and no one ever did. No matter what the situation might be in his life, he confronted it straight up. He was a real cat who carried himself with pride and knowledge. Tis could talk about things that other young men his age wouldn't know anything about. He constantly read books of many dimensions while sitting around the house. Tis could tell you about cultural differences going on in the Middle East as well as explain to the laymen why the axis of the earth moved the way it moved. He was only a few years older than me, but he was very impressionable.

As I struggled against his grip, he calmed me by shaking me, then he whispered to me as to why I wasn't home eating at the dinner table. Who wanted me home on a Saturday evening when Shawna was out playing hot peas and butter? Another hard shake of the collar snapped me out of that thinking process. I quickly explained to him that the time had passed quickly while playing. He turned around to see that all my friends were watching us and released my collar. That was Tis. If he thought that he was embarrassing me, he would immediately rectify the situation. He told me to go tell my friends that my mother was sick and I had to come home to take care of her. It was a lie, of course, but Tis knew I couldn't just be dragged away without the sight of it, making me look weak in the eyes of friends. Tis could analyze like that when it came to uncomfortable circumstances. I walked over to my friends and told them the lie Tis had created for me. Shawna looked pained as I explained the situation. She even asked me if I wanted her to walk with us home. I looked at that marvelous breast, licked my lips, and then glanced at my brother who was giving me a mean stare down. I declined her offer, but told her I will see her in school.

As Tis and I began our journey home, thoughts of Shawna stayed with me. While walking, I heard Tis laughing beside me. He wanted to know why I did not grab the belt. I looked at him quizzically. He said that he had been standing there for a while watching us play. I informed him that I could not hit

Shawna, she was a girl. And anyway, I liked her a lot. Tis laughed harder. Between breaths, he explained to me that I should keep that philosophy of not hitting girls as I grew older. I did not know what he meant then; he placed his brotherly arm around my shoulder as we continued walking, telling me that real men like your father don't have to hit women to get their point across. Real men know how to love their women with respect and treat her like a queen.

When we arrived home twenty minutes later, I was greeted with sour expressions from my mother and father. Evelyn shrugged when our eyes met. She, being the little sister, always took my side. Probably since we were so close in age and the fact that we look so much alike. We weren't twins, but everyone that met us for the first time knew by the resemblance that we were brother and sister. I adored Evelyn; she was funny, smart, and a leader. She could make you laugh by saying and doing the silliest things. In any family, you need a tension breaker when confronted by strenuous situations. There where many times growing up when I was about to be disciplined by my father for something crazy, and Evelyn would save me by placing herself between my father and me. Evelyn was the pride of the house, my father's only daughter; my father would not dare hit her, not even by mistake, and Evelyn knew this and she was spoiled rotten. This would often result in a verbal lashing instead of the pounding of his calloused hand against my backside. After a quick reprimand for me being out, my father told me to wash my hands and sit. Out the corner of my eye, I would give Evelyn a wink.

Having dinner at my house was like a competitive test of who could tell the most interesting stories that had happened during the week. My mother always seemed to have the funniest stories. Most of her stories stemmed from her girlfriends their husbands and children. My mother was the typical housewife. She was five feet and five inches in height but walked tall in our home.

She always had her hands manicured, and her hair was always done. She'd prepare our dinner. Do our homework with us while ironing clothing for school for several days in advance. Mom was from the South, and she conducted herself in that fashion. If you wronged her, she'd wrong you back tenfold, but if you treated her with respect and kindness, she did the same.

I had to be about seven or eight years old when one of my friends took some candy from me in school. He and I fought that day, and I was taken to the principal's office while he was let go because his mother was on the PTA board. That's parents who sit down with other parents to discuss how they can make things in the school better for the children. Well, when my mother found this out, she marched straight to the principal's office the next day and verbally ripped out his jugular vein with words I didn't know she possessed. I sat there and was amazed at how this strong, motherly, black woman displayed her love for her child and the obvious unfairness administered by the principal. She demanded that she meet with the mother of the boy who took my candy. Yes, we fought, but the boy was fifteen pounds heavier than I was and I gave it all I had; my dad instilled in me early to protect myself at all costs. When my mother saw my swollen lip and my black eyes, her eyes turned red with anger. For most of the night, I heard her shouting at my father; my father tried to reason with her by telling her that boys will be boys, but my mother was not trying to hear any of that. Eventually though, the mother of the boy who took my candy decided that she would rather have my mother as an ally rather than an enemy so she pulled some strings and my mother was voted into the PTA. Go, Mom.

Tis and I shared a room as brothers growing up. So there were many nights when I would lie in bed and tell him my life direction. Growing up in a less than glittery neighborhood, we were surrounded by older boys thinking of getting into the drug game, doing house and store burglaries, or becoming stick-up boys. Let me remind you, this was when I was eight years old! Facing outstanding peer pressure, your average child, a minority, is thinking of getting out of the deep, dark ghetto at an early age. Yet around every corner, there is someone whispering in your ear that they have a plan to make your life better. That plan almost always derives from a criminal intent, designed to entrap you into a life of crime leading to death or prison.

In America, the American Dream is the beautiful white house, picket white fence, two kids, the beautiful woman, and of course, the cute little dog. This is what you're told as a child. However, a child living in the dredges of the ghetto is thinking of getting out by doing anything and everything to ensure they get out, at least in thought. If it meant robbing, stealing, shooting, or stabbing someone to make it happen, then that's the direction one took. There are no illusions of grandeur living in the ghetto. It is what it is and a little bit more. I was aware of my surroundings, and no matter how many times I might've tried to ignore my conditions and the social ills engulfing my community, there was always a shootout or a bloody sidewalk to remind me, and if I did not find an outlet to something positive, what would my future have in store for me?

Tis would tell me that society looked at young boys like him and me and think we wouldn't live past the age of nineteen. We would either become statistics of the streets, prison, or a funeral home. Tis could be brutal with his outlook concerning the life we were living, but considering the hard lessons of life that we see on a daily basis, it had to be the only way.

Let me give you a psychological breakdown of a young male growing up in an environment where the police is resented and hated because they are deemed to be evil and brutal by their direct assault and disrespect toward those of color. Most police officers are born outside the main boroughs of New York City. They go to mostly white schools where they see the misrepresentation of people of color on television and the movies. Worse, we can also include many news organizations that create this image whenever they show brutal events while reporting on the urban neighborhoods. My family was from the south and their sentiments of the police were no different. Yet my parents insisted that if we played by the rules that are expected of us, the police would respect you as an individual. Sure, we struggled, but there was always love in my home, and through that love of God and family, I found my own self-importance as a young black male.

The projects was an entire different scene from what I was accustomed to; people were all on top of each other, eighteen floors and ten apartments on each floor. Everybody seemed to not care about anything except themselves—at least I thought that at first.

My first encounter in the Albany Projects had to do with a young man by the name of Choke. Man, he was about fourteen or fifteen years old and stood about five feet eleven inches. He wasn't a handsome boy, but what he lacked in looks, he made up for in his clothing. He always had the latest wears in style clothing, shoes, and sneakers. He had every Kangol that you could imagine and in every color. Most people revered this young hoodlum who demanded respect by his sheer, powerful aura and the fact that he was making money.

Now you might be asking yourself, why is his name Choke? Well, I don't think that his parents named him that at birth, but to this day and unbeknown to me, I would find out his actual name later in life, which made me laugh. Anyway, I am leading you down this road to enlighten you on how a fourteen-year-old could be envied in the projects. Have you ever heard of the Dope Fiend Yoke? No? If not, let me give you…hmm, a brief description of this title. The Dope Fiend Yoke is simply that. In the urban world, we try to put a title on everything to make it more colorful. For example, Dope Fiend is a heroin addict. Yoke is a person placing a forearm across the opposite arm and squeezing—not pulling the person's larynx into your body—until the person is unconscious. Choke became a dope fiend yoke specialist around the Albany Projects. He would wait until the first of the month and the middle of the month when people received either their Social Security, disability, or public assistance checks after they've been cashed and he would set out to get as many as he could. One day in the summer of 1980, a few of my new friends and I were hanging out on the corner of St. Marks Avenue when Choke and a few of his boys walked up to us.

Man, I am not easily intimidated. I have never ran into a person where I felt that I had to bow down to for any reason, but when I saw Choke, I realize that this young, strong dude was going to try me. He would try me because I was the new kid on the block, and he had to see where my strengths and weaknesses lie. I always had some kind of intuition ever since I was a kid. It was like I could look at a person and know they were schemers. They used their intimidation to make others do their dirty work. Choke was one of those who had others lapping at his heels because he was getting money at the age of fourteen. He was a leader, and he led with his money and his threats. At the moment he glanced at me, I knew he was going to try me. My man, Zo, whispered in my ear, "Hold your own, Shan." Shan was my nickname given to me by my brother Tis. I didn't understand what Zo meant at the time, but I had a feeling that something was going down, and Zo, being a kid I had met about a month earlier in school, pulled my coat to Choke. Zo lived in my building. He was a skinny kid, but his fist was what gave him his respect. He was fifteen and had started boxing at the gym. His fist talked for him, and when they did, the person who wanted to hear them usually would be staring at Zo from the ground with a bloody lip. I don't know why we clicked when we met, but he was like a comedian. He told the craziest jokes that made you cry with laughter. At the moment though, no one was laughing as we watched Choke and his hoodlum friends approach.

"What's up, Zo? " Choke said. Zo nodded.

"Somebody new?" Choke asked.

I knew if I didn't speak up and stand my own ground, I was going to be thought of as soft. And let me tell you, living in the projects and being thought of as soft is not something you want to be labeled as. You see, if I would have shown any sense of fear, one iota of fear, then I would be a piece of meat on the streets of Brooklyn, waiting to be constantly challenged and intimidated by anyone that came in contact with me. No matter how I might try to avoid the confrontation, it wouldn't have mattered to those making an intimidating move against me. There would always be someone waiting in the shadows to try me. To goad me. Choke, although I wouldn't know it then, would be my sounding board to present to the world.

"Hey, what's up? My name is Shan. I just moved here from Bedstuy. I like your Kangol. It's a different color. I had the opportunity of watching you do your thing a few weeks ago against that dude you were talking to. I don't know how you put him down like that, but I was impressed."

"So you and Zo are good people, huh?" Choke asked and I nodded. My eyes never left Choke. We stared at each other for a good three seconds. Finally when he blinked and looked away, I knew I had set the stage for my dominance of the situation by him breaking eye contact.

"You cats want to hang out with us?" Choke asked.

"We have some girls we're going to meet at the train station in a few minutes," Zo said.

Choke looked from Zo to me. He arched his eyebrows as if our answer wasn't truthful. "Where are these girls from?" he asked.

"Marcy Projects," I said before Zo could answer.

"What are their names?" Choke asked.

Zo shrugged. "You know," he began as he looked around nonchalantly. Lashera Maleria, something like that."

"You mean Lameshia," Choke asked, as a smile slowly formed on his large lips and his eyes twinkled.

I looked at Zo. We both nodded in agreement and looked back at Choke.

It seemed like the air around me became hot as I stared at Choke. His expression was deadpan serious. I knew if it came to a fight, I couldn't let him put me in the Dope Fiend Yoke. If he did, I would be the laughing stock of Albany Projects for letting him choke me out. I had a little boxing knowledge that my brother Tis had been teaching me, but I only weighed one hundred and twenty pounds soaking wet, and Choke was well over one hundred and seventy pounds. Yet I would use those skills to the best of my knowledge rather than get caught out there, looking like a clown in a neighborhood that fed off others' faults and weaknesses.

Choke turned and looked at the young boys who'd come with him. He whispered something to them, and they all began laughing. I blinked while licking my lips. I had already evaluated where the situation was leading and what I had to do. Realizing it now, I'd always been able to see things before the picture was entirely in front of me. Don't ask me to explain it in words. It was just something I could always do.

Choke was coming for a fight. If he made any threatening move toward me, then I would make the second move by doing my best to knock his ass out with all my strength. I took a step back and waited. Zo, having a sense of dread, I guess, did the same. Sure, he could've been diabolical and stepped away from me and saved face, but he instead stepped with me, letting me know that however it went down, he would be on my side.

"Hey, man," Choke said, as he turned back around toward us. "We know Lameshia. She's worth the wait and more."

He began laughing as he walked away followed by his small cutthroat henchman. They glanced back from time to time as they continued walking away.

"Whew," Zo sighed. "I thought we were going to go at them some kind of hard. Choke is not someone to be taken lightly. If he would've raised his hands against us, we would have been fighting till the next day."

I nodded in agreement.

"I hear besides him and his people ganging up and choking people out, they're also becoming stick-up kids throughout Brooklyn. They're throwing guns in people's faces and taking everything they have. And, I hear, he doesn't care who it is. Being around them is like being a magnet for bullets," Zo said.

"Yeah, those bullets are hot. And bullets don't discriminate," I said. "Where did you come up with those names, man? That was quick. You can think on your feet."

"I don't know, but I would rather be quick in the mind than be choked out and lying on the ground," Zo said, as he glanced at me.

"He wouldn't have done that to you. Maybe against me because I'm new in the neighborhood, but not you. You could've walked away. He knows you."

"Come on, man. Why would I do that, Shan? You're a good dude. Anyway, if I would've walked away, he would've thought I was a punk and tried me next. This way if we both stand our ground, then he has the two of us to deal with instead of one. That's loyalty in its fullest form, brother." No doubt.

It was at that moment that I knew what the word *loyalty* meant. How it was defined and how it should be used. Some people can say it, and it doesn't mean anything. It was the word in itself that I came to cherish as I grew older, and it would be something that I would hold dear to my heart and consciousness.

By the end of the year, my father had decided to move out. That was a blow to me as a young man who'd grown up living with a two-parent household. I was a young boy who adored his father and respected him for being a man in a society where black men were looked upon as lazy, unfeeling, abusive, and who abandoned their children. My father, Fred, had none of those traits, and I loved him for that. He and my mother had decided on an amicable and mutual separation. They both agreed on a monetary understanding regarding me, my brother, and my sister every month that ensured her he would be there for us. His decision to move out was not abandonment or another woman. He and my mother were involved with each other for over twenty- five years. And like every relationship, we fall in love at one point in our lives, and eventually, we fall out of love. It is the cycle of life. I don't think either my father or mother blamed the other for the ending of the relationship. Time has a way of making us evaluate our lives and the one we are spending it with. A deterioration of love could best describe it.

Although my father had moved out and found his own place in Brooklyn, he was in contact with me, my sister, and my brother. He made it a point to be there for birthdays, family events, and other family functions. His presence ensured us all that he was not totally out of our lives. It was this act that made me see the difference between a man and a black man. Is there a difference, you ask?

Absolutely.

First, understand the difficulty of a black man trying to exist in America back in that era. He is confronted with negativity to the point of losing his mind, and in some circumstances, some black men have snapped and gone on a rampage of killing, abandonment, physical abuse of their spouse, or other unlimited emotional hang-ups. Psychologists delve in the mind of these men, seeking clinical reasoning as to what made these men snap. Would the fact that these men endured a lifetime of discrimination, alienation, and the indoctrination of slavery have anything to do with it? Yes, I could go on writing page after page about why black men have their limitations in regard to society, but then I would not be able to finish this book.

As for the concept of a *man*, we go into how a man is defined. The average man not of color has a simple life. He has the freedom of the world and the choice to achieve great things that he shares with his family and community. He walks with his chest out, knowing he can fulfill his dreams and not be singled out. He has unlimited access to the things in life that a man of color doesn't. That's the difference. I proclaim to be a *man*.

When 1984 rolled in, I was out living up my passion in the clubs throughout the city on Friday and Saturday nights, working the dance floor with some breathtaking, beautiful woman. It was my outlet. I worked during the week and enjoyed myself on the weekends. I wasn't into other things like some of my friends were into, like selling drugs on the block, hoping to get rich quick. Or the grab and rob tactics in the projects, nor was I into the pimping of young girls that suddenly became the craze for guys my age. Some guys my age fed off that kind of atmosphere in my neighborhood. I morally refused to become apart of that environment. All these things I saw and knew about but refused to participate in that dark, ravishing world.

I felt that if I did, I would lose myself in a pit of debauchery. The part-time job that I was doing supplied me with some money and let me buy the little things my mother couldn't afford to get me or my father, who believed in young men my age fending for themselves. And if being a man meant responsibility, then he wanted me to stand for myself without doing an act of crime to get money. My parents had taught me to be respectful to myself as well as others, and it was these conscious efforts that made me stay away from guys my age that were doing long, hard time or were killed before reaching the age of eighteen, and I, no different than them in the color spectrum, refuse to become one of those statistics.

I wanted to give you an image of my mentality at this young age because this conversation is leading up to a more in-depth story. Remember, I told you that I enjoyed dancing. Well, one Friday night in the summer of that year, I was preparing myself to go to the Roxy Club in Manhattan. Whoa. The music was hot! The young women and men always wore the latest style in clothing, and the people danced to the sound of that era. Man, I had gotten off work that evening and taken a nap to build up my dancing stage legs for later that night. When I woke up about ten o'clock that night, I heard a knock at my door—actually my mother's door—I went to answer it. It was Drew.

Have you ever met someone you wanted to hang out with but didn't want to really be with in public? You know what I mean, right? Well, that was Drew, short, brown skin, always angry because his mother wouldn't give him money whenever he wanted it, and his father, to everyone's surprise, was now messing around with his aunt who is the mother's half-sister. He was living a complicated life, and I felt sorry for him. So besides his anger issues, he's also consumed with trying to be the "man" in the neighborhood. At that moment though, as he squeezed his way into my mother's apartment, he was trying to convince me to hang out with him and his cousin, Darlene. That wasn't going to happen tonight, I thought. His cousin Darlene was from North Carolina, and she had the most ear-shrieking laughter ever heard. Whenever she laughed, I blinked while shaking my head. She wasn't the prettiest catch, but what she lacked in beauty, she gained in physical thickness. She was sixteen, and she possessed a body that was like a grown woman. She had it all: breasts, thighs, and an unbelievable butt that stuck out no matter how she tried to hide it. If it wasn't for her crazy laugh and her thick Southern accent, I might've been interested in her.

"So what's up, Shan, you hanging tonight?" Drew asked, as he rushed into the living room and sat down on the sofa without an invitation.

I followed him into the living room. I stared at him while shaking my head in disbelief. Drew had no class, I thought. He could never take a hint that he was overstaying his welcome.

"Hey, Darlene wanted me to ask you," Drew began, as he looked around, "your Mom got new furniture?'

I walked over to the chair in the corner and sat down. "Man, I am not messing with you and your cousin, Darlene. Last time we did our thing together, she nearly had us fighting in the Chinese restaurant with some of those boys from Marcy Projects. What would make her act like she liked the boy, and then when we were leaving, she want to act all high society on him. Your cousin is a tease."

"Yeah, I talked to her about that. She has a Southern attitude when it comes to boys, and in her mind, she thought that was cute," Drew said. "Shan, she brought some chunky black up from the woods. You know that stuff burns good." Drew smiled.

"Come on, man, you know I don't smoke that crap," I said with anger. "Every time I see you, you want to smoke trees. I hear you're not going to school anymore. Is that true? You need to give up the smoking and concentrate on getting your life together."

Drew shrugged. "You know me and the situation with my mom. I feel embarrassed whenever I go to school with last year's clothing, man. I keep wearing sneakers from two years ago. My mother has no understanding of my feelings toward my appearance. When I try to explain to her how I feel, she shrugs me off and tells me that I need to think of other things in my life."

"Get a job! " I snapped as I leaped out of my chair. "You are no different than me. I work after school and on the weekends at the hardware store, and every time I ask you if you want me to speak up for you in getting you a job, you act like I'm talking a foreign language, man. You have to make your own moves in this world. Your mother is on welfare, she's working off the books to make a little extra money, and you don't help with your bitching, man! Get it together." I shook my head. I was disgusted with Drew's selfish attitude.

Drew nodded as he stared at me.

I turned and walked out of the room to start getting ready for the club.

"So…you don't want to hang out with me and my cousin and smoke some chunky black?" Drew asked. I looked at him like he done lost his damn mind. "This is some good smoke. It'd make you choke on the inhale."

No! Man, I will see you later. Let me walk your ass to the door. You are driving me crazy with this smoking weed bullshit. Have you thought about getting some help with your disease?" I asked.

He looked at me with a questionable stare. "Ah, right. Ah, right, "Drew said as he stood up. "I'm outta here. I will tell Darlene you had to work and can't hang with us. But I think she likes you."

I watched Drew walk to the door.

"Yeah, well, you tell her to hold on to those thoughts," I said.

When Drew went out the door, I laughed. The boy refuses to accept any rejection. In his mind, everyone smoked.

𝕾𝖜𝖊𝖊𝖙 𝕸𝖚𝖘𝖎𝖈

(Winter 1986)

When I arrived at the club that night, it was about twelve o'clock in the morning, and I was feeling good, smelling good, and looking good. Not that I want to sound conceited or anything by this description. I'm simply stating the facts at the time. Now you might be wondering how I could get access into the club at the age of sixteen, and worse, why was my mother letting me hang out so late. First, I knew the security guard at the door. Well, he knew a lady in my building named Irma, who he was trying to get with, and I knew Irma from going to the store for her from time to time. Anyway, we met one day in my building and we were tight ever since. Secondly, of course, my mother didn't know I was going out to clubs. I would tell her that I was going over to Zo's house to spend the night. Zo's mother had met my mother, and they clicked with a motherly friendship. Those Friday and Saturday nights also gave me the opportunity to sneak over to Kelly's apartment. Who is Kelly? I will talk about her before the night is over. Right now though, let me fill you in on my clubbing scene, and the fire of the music when it touched my ears.

"Music brings about a sense of calmness in me. I can have the most stressful week, and when I go into a club, man…I feel like the world is behind me." That I'd entered a cocoon of solace.

The music is pulsating through my soul, my mind, my fingers; everywhere on my body, there is a tingling sensation with every beat. The women, as I glanced around, were many and beautiful as they walked around smelling good and looking mesmerizing. No matter how many times I walk into a club, it always would feel like it was my first time. I mean except for the cigarette smoke destroying the ambiance, everything else was cool. I went to the center of the dance floor with a cup of soda in my hand and watched the scene unfold as the young men and women brought their best dance moves for the world to see. I loved it! There's nothing like a beautiful woman in a short, leather skirt, black four-inch heels, and a silky black blouse dancing alone to the sound of the music. Hips are swaying, and their drinks constantly spilling. Most of these women were older than me by at least five or six years, but that didn't stop me from asking them to dance, and it was a rarity if I were turned down. I would dance from the moment I walked into the dark, dank, smoke-filled atmosphere until they were turning on the lights and kicking everyone out. The night was mine and I was going to enjoy it to the fullest… and much more. I looked around for my three home girls who I chilled with on occasion: Linda, Penny, and Stephanie to make sure they were safe and then I left.

Five hours later, I sat in the back of the cab heading back to Brooklyn; I was smiling. I'd danced until my feet were hurting, but I had several telephone numbers to bring me comfort from some beautiful women who were a little older than me, and my smile grew bigger as the image of Kelly popped in my mind. Kelly was twenty-four years old. Is that a shocker to you? Well, it is not. I met her one day walking down the street on Nostrand Avenue about six months ago. She'd ignored my open advances of conversation as I walked beside her that day. She kept telling me "I was too young to be talking to her." Yet my persistency wore her down to the point that she took my number and called me about two weeks later. Now, as I lingered in the back of the cab, I felt a feeling of joy. Tonight was going to be the night—morning really—that Kelly was going to let me see her apartment.

Twenty minutes later, I was standing in front of her apartment door. She lived on Tillery Street. It was a three-floor walk up. At that moment, I didn't care if it was a ten-floor walk up; I was going to make it to her door and kick off my shoes. My feet were killing me. As I stood there deciding on whether to knock or call it a night, the door opened and my decision to leave flew out of my thought process as I stared at Kelly standing in the doorway.

At sixteen, you're used to seeing girls your own age, and most of their mentalities are "sixteen." As I stared at Kelly standing in the doorway wearing a red negligee and a pair of red silk stockings and red open-toe six-inch heel pumps, my heart nearly fell into my stomach. Here was a woman in the purest sense of the word. Her skin glistened with moisture, and the perfume she was wearing nearly made me fall to my knees as it wafted through my open nose. I felt myself groan from the sight of her. It was a groan of astonishing, blood-rushing lust. Her hair was cut short below her ears. Her fully exposed breasts appeared to topple her over because of their size. Her lovely, thick thighs made me sigh in anticipation. She was an older woman who cared for herself with pride, and that impressed me.

"Do you want to stand out there until the afternoon, Anthony, or would you like to come in?" Kelly asked as she took a step back out of the doorway.

"Uh."

"You've been talking so much about what you were going to do to me if I give you the chance. Well…here's your chance. Don't tell me the young man has become bashful like a little boy when he sees a woman standing in front of him," Kelly remarked.

"What? Huh?" was all that I could think of to say. I was at loss of words, but my eyes kept staring at her from head to toe, and then back to head, and finally resting on her breasts. "Anthony, come in. It will be okay," Kelly urged soothingly, as she gently reached out and grabbed my hand.

Man, I stumbled, stuttered, and damn near cried with happiness when Kelly pulled me into her apartment. When she closed the door behind me, I felt a sense of euphoria. A feeling I can't explain unless you've experienced it as a sixteen-year-old. I was dancing as she led me to her bedroom. When I left her apartment, my outlook on older women had changed considerably. There was a sense of learning the wants and needs of an older woman that made me feel wanted. No. Let me correct that: it was a feeling of being needed that made me appreciate the beauty of them inside out. I didn't know it then, but it would be the exposure that would set my taste for older woman on a higher level.

Would that encounter with Kelly be considered sexual abuse of a minor? I always thought about that question while getting older, and I refuse to say that it did. That experience at sixteen wasn't abuse to me in the sense of the word, but a form of teaching. I learned that the sexual needs of a woman were more profound than a man's, and she showed me, with time and practice that my wants and desires should be secondary to hers. I never questioned her outlook on the matter.

Why should I? She was treating me like a king with all the benefits of an older man.

The things she taught me, I would carry over into my future relationships with women regardless of their age.

By the time 1986 rolled in, I was comfortable with my life. I had no real self-doubts and I had come to accept the loss of my brother Tis to the penal system that touches every urban, young, black male. It pains me to even comment on my brother's situation. I speak briefly on it to simply enlighten you as to my not mentioning him anymore while telling my story. Like every family of color, we have circumstances that are beyond our control. My brother's situation is no different. He'd found himself in a situation that resulted in him choosing to raise his hand or lose his life. In circumstances like that, your options are very limited. Let's just say he had to do what he had to do without regret.

My mother had decided to go back to school a few years earlier to get a bachelor's degree in social service. Well, my sister and I tended to find other means to fill the void in our lives. Most of the time, my sister and I did our thing whenever my mother was at school or working. Evelyn was a good cook at fifteen, so we had that family setting still continuing in the evening. We grew up quickly once my mother started going back to school. It wasn't bad, mind you. It was different. I had started seeing Kelly three times a week. We'd grown comfortable with our relationship. In the first three months, she'd wanted to break off our sexual thing and be friends. At first, I protested, but who was I to protest? She showed me things no other woman would dare contemplate. I respected her wish, and for two weeks, I didn't call her. I was sixteen years old, and I wasn't arrogant about it. She was fun to be with, and I didn't want to jeopardize our friendship.

Her sexual needs were a different story altogether, though. By the third week, she called me and admitted that she'd missed me and that we should have lunch the next day. Who am I to act like I didn't miss her? Not just the sex, but her fun ways and silly humor as well. She could tell a joke and keep the punch line until the right moment to spring it. I liked her. You could tell where this lunch date went, am I right? Before the month was over, Kelly and I were back to doing our thing as if we'd never been apart.

Whenever I met a girl in my neighborhood, she would tell me she'd heard about me from some other girl. I didn't know whether to feel honored or ashamed. But like everything as to the outlook of a sixteen-year-old, I shook it off. I was happy. I had an older woman who worshipped the ground I walked on, and I had come into my own while living in Albany Projects. I had become a person that others respected simply in the way I conducted myself. It was through my calm demeanor and the way I handled situations between others that ensured that I was someone to be reckoned with. I showed respect when needed, and I demanded respect when confronted. This is the concept of living in the projects. Be a jackal with big teeth or become someone that others jacked and abused. I refuse to be anyone's victim. That's the greatest thing my father had taught me, with his strong Southern Native American tradition: protect yourself and your family at all cost.

One late winter evening, while lying in bed beside Kelly, I had a bad feeling in my stomach for a few days. I couldn't put my finger on it. I was waking up feeling nauseous, and some evenings, I would go to bed early. I felt tired all the time no matter how much sleep I might've gotten. I thought about telling my mother about it, but I knew if I did, she would demand that I stay in the house until she could take me to see a doctor. I didn't want to see the doctor or have her hovering over me like a baby, so I continued to put it off.

"How was your day today?" Kelly asked me.

I turned toward her. She was naked, and the room smelled of sex. She'd shown me a new trick with her tongue, and it had made my toes curl. She'd shown me things in bed that made me more attractive to her. I was still learning about a woman's body, and she gave me one-on-one teaching lessons. I would ask the question, and she would perform the answers for me on my body. She was a warm woman who didn't treat me like I was sixteen.

"I haven't seen my period in two weeks," Kelly said as she rolled over and looked at me while stroking my hairless chest.

I smiled. "Where was the last place you saw it?" I said, as I laughed at my lame joke while gently caressing her breast. "Did you leave it at a friend's house?"

Kelly playfully slapped me on my arm and smiled. "You're funny," she said. "Anyway, no period means what?"

"It means…" I said, letting the question hang in the air.

"I think I'm pregnant, Anthony," Kelly said.

My smile disappeared. I stared at her as my mouth fell open in shock. What does that mean? I ask myself. The room began to spin a little as I ingested her words. I think my heart skipped a few beats as well.

"Are you with me, Anthony?" Kelly asked. She snapped her fingers in front of my face. "Is this too much for you?"

I sat up in bed. I looked around the room. It was as if I were seeing it for the first time. Pregnant? How the hell do I tell my mother that one? I asked myself. Yet the sickness I'd been feeling has suddenly disappeared.

"Listen, I know this is real heavy on you right now, Anthony. You're young, and sometimes, when you play with adults, adult things happen, and this is one of them. I know not to expect much from you. I want to keep this baby. I've had problems in the past with getting pregnant, and I know this baby may be my last one. I need you to understand that I didn't set out to get pregnant, but things happen. You don't have to worry about caring for the baby. I—"

"What! Do you think that I would let you go through this by yourself?" I asked her, as I turned toward her. "Don't underestimate me because I'm young. It's our child, and I will be there for my firstborn. Sure, it's new to me, but that doesn't stop me from being involved in the raising of my child! Do you want to get married?"

Kelly stared at me. I guess the way I responded shocked her. She nodded and then smiled. "I always knew there was something special about you, Anthony," she said as she hugged me. When she pulled away, she was smiling. "I don't think getting married to a sixteen-year-old is legal, but thank you for asking."

I sat there staring at the wall in front of me as I felt the warmth of Kelly's body against mine. I was going to be a father. The world had changed on me in a matter of minutes, and at that moment, I grew up a little more. I wanted to laugh and cry at the same time, but for what? That wouldn't change a thing. Not one thing at all. How was I going to tell my mother? Very discreetly, I thought, and from a distance in which she wouldn't be to close to reach out to grab me.

Nine months later, I was in the hospital, nervously pacing back and forth as I waited for the birth of my child. After months of doctor's visit with Kelly for prenatal care, I was ready for this baby's arrival. Nurses would walk by me and ask if I were Kelly's little brother. I would proudly raise my chin and state with the youth of arrogance that I was the father. They gave me a dubious stare as they'd walk away with a look of disbelief. Sure, I knew it was something different. A young boy having a baby at my age with a woman much older than him in today's moral world. Would I like to run away from it? Abandon my responsibilities to my child and the mother? Absolutely not. What kind of person would I be? I could not live that way. The fact that I had a father in my life that raised me was influential in my decision. What if my father had left my mother? What would've been my outcome in life? I was having a baby. And if it took my last breath, I would raise my child, guide my child in life, and love my child with all my heart. If I never gave my child anything, he or she would have my love to keep them strong.

I was in a deep sleep on the waiting area couch when I felt someone gently touching my arm. I opened my eyes to see an elderly woman standing over me, smiling. I sat up and felt a rush from lack of sleep overtake me. I steadied myself as I blinked rapidly to clear my vision.

"Are you here waiting for news of the arrival of a baby from Kelly Brokins?" she asked me.

I rubbed the crust out of my eyes and blinked twice. I nodded.

"I'm Dr. Wilkins. Your sister has had a baby girl. I guess that makes you a proud uncle," she said.

My heart skipped two beats as I stared at the doctor. "A girl? She's a girl? Is she healthy? She's not sick, right?" I said all of this in one sentence.

"Your niece is well," Dr. Wilkins said.

I smiled. "She's my daughter," I said, as pride filled my heart. Dr. Wilkins took a step back.

I stood up. My chest was swollen. "She's my daughter, and I'm going to name her Monique," I said.

Dr. Wilkins stared at me. She smiled. "That's a beautiful name. Congratulations," she said. "Give it another hour and someone will come out and take you in to see your…"

"My girlfriend?" I said.

"Yes, your girlfriend," Dr. Wilkins said, as she smiled and walked away.

I watched her hurriedly walk away. I closed my eyes as I laid my head back against the back of the chair. I had created life, and now I had to be responsible and caring in regard to raising that life. There was no gray area in this, I knew that.

There were only solid facts. I had stepped over the threshold of innocent young man and into the zone of adult and fatherhood. I had become a man. Fearful as it might've seem, I knew that there was no other option in regard to my daughter. She was my firstborn, my legacy of things to come. Her birth had placed on my shoulders her continued existence, and to do that, I would make sure she had everything she might need in life. I was making a promise to myself to ensure that she did well, if it took the last breath in my body.

Four months later, I was in Kelly's apartment, bouncing my daughter on my knees. She was beautiful with fat cheeks and a warm smile. Every time I bounced her, she would giggle hysterically. Her gaiety was breathtaking.

"Have you told your family about your child yet?" Kelly shouted from the kitchen. She was preparing a bottle for Monique.

"I told my mother and sister," I said as I tickled my daughter's chubby chin and watched her giggle some more. "My mother is still a little…angry. You know grandmothers. She wanted to be there at birth and is thinking I didn't do right by her as to not letting her know that you were pregnant. Little things like that, you know."

Kelly walked into the living room with the bottle. She snatched Monique out of my arms like a protective lioness engulfing her child from danger. I looked at her confused as I cocked my head to the side, waiting for her to explain herself.

"Your mother doesn't like me," Kelly said, as she sat in the chair in the far corner cradling Monique and giving me the evil eye.

"What do you want from me? I can't make my mother like you. In her mind, she thinks you manipulated me or seduced me or something like that. She keeps calling you a harlot or a cougar, whatever that means," I said. "I told her it was something that I did willingly. And I was having fun while doing it."

"Don't act like this is funny, Anthony. I'm serious. Since that baby been born, I've tried to connect with your mother, and she keeps shunning me. How do I work with that? If you told her in the very beginning, she wouldn't be having this dislike toward me," Kelly asked, as she stared at me waiting for an answer.

"What do you want me to do, make my mother like you? My mother is stubborn in her own way. Even if she knew early on about you being pregnant, she would've done things her own way. She does what she does. Give her time, she'll come around," I said. "Even if she doesn't, I'm still here, and that's what matters."

Kelly smiled as she glanced at me. "I should still be angry with you, but you rationalized things so plainly that it throws me off. How is school?"

"School is fine. I have a class that I have to concentrate on in the next three weeks, but other than that, everything is everything," I said, as I avoided Kelly's stare. "Listen, I have to go to work in about two hours. Is there anything you want me to get for the baby before I leave?"

"How are you working two jobs and going to school?" Kelly asked.

"It's working out. Don't worry. I'm good," I said, as I stood up and walked toward her. I kissed her and my daughter. "Everything is okay."

"It better be," Kelly said with a smile, as I closed the door behind me. I gave a quick glance behind me. I saw that Kelly was staring hard at me. I smiled as I continued to close the door.

Like everything that is good in a relationship in the beginning, it's all sweet and fun, but when the situation arises, like the birth of my daughter, things became more serious. Kelly had faded from a sexy woman to a concerned mother, making sure the father of her child was stable. I wasn't angry at her. I respect that. To me, she appeared to be caring for her child—our child—and she did that by ensuring that I was doing the right thing. Our intimacy had disappeared since the arrival of Monique. Was I angry? No. To me, it displayed Kelly's motherhood in a fine form.

As I walked back to my mother's home, I was thinking hard about Kelly's questioning my being in school, though. I hadn't been to school consistently in three days. My mother didn't know. My sister did. Evelyn picked up on me being tired all the time. We had always been close, so I didn't lie to her about me taking on another job to help support Kelly and the baby. It was my job to do as much as possible to ensure that my child was taken care of. Anything less than that would be me neglecting my fatherhood, and I couldn't accept that possibility.

There was no one home when I walked into the house an hour later. I went to my room and fell on my bed. My thoughts were full as I stared at the ceiling. Man, what was I going to do?

In my mind, I thought I was handling things fairly well. I made sure my child had formula, Pampers, and clothing. I was there when she had her first doctor's appointment and all. Why wasn't I feeling complete?

"This is where you've been hiding out?"

I turn toward my doorway. My sister Evelyn was standing there, holding a bag. She'd just came in from shopping at the supermarket. We looked so much alike that people thought we were twins. She was a good sister and I adored her.

"Not hiding out, just thinking some things out, sis. How was school?" Evelyn gave me a cross look as she walked farther into my room. She stood over me. "School was that bad, huh?" I asked and then smiled.

"I haven't seen you in school in minutes," Evelyn said.

That would be true, I admitted, considering we went to the same school and would see each other in the corridor between changing classes. All I could do was nod.

"Are you dropping out of school?" Evelyn asked me.

"No," I said as I sat up. "I'm just trying to do right by my daughter."

"Do you think your daughter would appreciate it if you killed yourself working two jobs and sleeping less and less as the weeks go on? Worse, do you think Mom would like your baby mama even more if she knew you were killing yourself working the way you do?"

"Mom is not helping the situation by not being grandmotherly to her grandchild. And what about Kelly's feelings? She won't even give the lady a chance to connect to her in a mother-in-law way. It's like I'm swimming upstream, and every time I get to shore, someone knocks me back into the water."

Evelyn smiled as I watched her walk toward my bed and sit down. She cradled the groceries on her lap as she stared at me. "You've been reading those Shakespearian and philosophical books again, haven't you? Writers like Aristotle and Plato, huh? Upstream stuff? Impressive."

I smiled. Yeah, my sister knew me well. "Evelyn, I don't understand what's up with our mother. She won't communicate with Kelly at all. She ignores her even when Kelly is trying to be respectful and courteous when she calls on the phone. It makes me upset that she shrugs her off like that even though the woman has had her grandchild. My first child!" I snapped furiously, as I sat up in bed and stared at my sister. "This is her first grandchild! Where is she coming from?"

My sister, always the patient one, the youngest, stared at me. I hated when she gave me that look of "Are you serious?" I thought she could look into my head when she did that.

"So let me get this right, Shan. You're upset with your mother because your baby mama, who is much older than you, feels that our mother is not showing her the proper respect in regard to the acknowledgement of your child being born as well as respect for herself, right?

I nodded.

"Now this woman, Kelly, has seduced you. Made you get her pregnant and now wants to play house with our mother after she has plucked a few nuts from you in a perverted kind of way. If this was reversed and a man had impregnated a sixteen-year-old female, what do you think would happen to him and how would he be labeled?"

I said nothing as I watched my sister wait patiently for me to answer.

"Can't think of anything, can you? Let me give you another scenario. Your daughter will be sixteen one day. She will come to you and inform you of some predator she met who is ten years older than she is, and with tears running down her face, she tells you she loves him and has been having sex with him. At sixteen! What is your reaction, bro?"

She had me. She was right. If it were reversed with my own child, I would resent the man who'd manipulated my child into falling into the throes of pre-adulthood. I would probably seek him out and do something ugly to him. My mother's attitude toward Kelly—from a woman's perspective—was right on point. How could she look at Kelly with respect, knowing the woman had sexually molested her sixteen-year-old son? I personally didn't feel molested. I felt very horny whenever I saw Kelly, but that's a young hormonal boy for you in the prime of his youth. We think with our little head. That thing that swings between our legs and makes decisions for us through lustful eyes and panting hearts. It dominates the big head on our shoulders when it comes to practical things of importance.

"You think I ought to keep some distance between our mother and Kelly?" I asked.

"That and get your ass back in school," Evelyn said as she stood up and headed to the door. "I have to get dinner started before Mama gets home. You're going to be all right?"

"I have no other choice but to be all right," I said with reluctance. "If I'm not all right, then no one is."

Evelyn laughed as she walked out of my room.

I lay back on my bed and began to let my thought process take effect as I wondered about what would be my next step. I had hit a bump in the road concerning my life. It was a bump that if not carefully worked out could one day leave a stain on my relationship with my mother, and I didn't want that. My mother was my foundation. My balance in life.

When winter came, it blew in with a frosty vengeance in Brooklyn. I was walking down St. Marks Avenue five months later on my way to Kelly's house. Kelly wanted to go out for dinner. By this time, I had completely left school altogether and concentrated on working to support my daughter. I had intercepted three letters from school that was addressed to my mother about my absenteeism.

One of the letters my sister had barely got to before my mother arrived home last week. What was I to do? Yes, I was wrong for skipping school to work, but how else was I going to support my daughter? For the past two months, I had been approached by the neighborhood drug dealers to join them in making money, selling cocaine and crack. I knew they're making unbelievable money in the dark world of sex, drugs, and money, but you can get so caught up in it and lose all morality. I'd seen too many young boys my age fall victim to the passion of making fast money, easy money, so they thought. There was nothing easy about becoming a pariah in a fish bowl full of guppies that is called the ghetto. Yet being tight for money can make a person have questionable thoughts as to their direction in life. The lack of its presence in life can make a person ignore their own like and dislikes; stomachs had to be fed. I was aware of this condition, but pushed it far from my consciousness. I refuse to let myself become a victim of my environment. To enslave myself to the dredges of a place that was unfeeling, irresponsible, and demeaning. No. The drug game was not for me. I didn't possess that brutality that was mandated to survive in that world. A world filled with more victims than conquerors.

After Kelly dropped the baby off at the babysitter, she and I boarded the train for downtown Brooklyn to eat dinner. She wanted to talk about where we were going in our relationship and how to better secure the future with our daughter. In other words, she was feeling neglected because I wasn't having sex with her as often since I'd been working two jobs. Kelly was a good woman, but I'd hit a boulder in my life where my daughter was concerned and it made me grow up very quickly, and there'd been discrepancies as to Kelly's actions. She seemed to always be agitated whenever I stopped over to visit. I also noticed that she'd taken up with a few dubious friends I thought were into some shady things, but I held my tongue…for now. I didn't want to put more of a strain on our current situation. We were both feeling a little stressful in different ways.

We both watched as the waiter took our orders. He was a young man who looked like he was working to pay his way through college. After a minute or two of Kelly's indecisiveness as to what she wanted to eat, he nodded his agreement and walked away. I had a few dollars in my pocket that evening and wanted to share some time with her. Although it was a problem getting those few dollars during the week, I had no hesitation in spending them on her. If it meant having the opportunity to be alone with Kelly, then I was good with that. She deserved a little attention in regard to caring for our baby and working.

"I'm glad we're out together having dinner, Anthony. I know we've been going through a lot lately with the baby and you working so much, but I appreciate you and having you in my life," Kelly said as she gently touched my hand.

I stared at her. Something was different about her. Her eyes looked glossy. I had noticed it on different occasions when I would come to her apartment unannounced. It was as if I'd interrupted her from doing something. She would act nervous. There was a faint aftersmell of something in the apartment whenever I walked around as well. I remember her always keeping her appearance in stellar condition. Her hair was always done as well as her fingernails. Lately though, there seemed to be some kind of change in her. I couldn't put my finger on it, but something was there…something was there calling out to me.

"You know the other day I was cleaning the kitchen and I heard the baby say Da-da. I was surprised," Kelly said. "Have you decided on coming to live with me yet? I'm not asking you to marry me. I just want to be…I don't know…have you close to us."

I stared at her. I'd never heard her talking about getting married before, where was this coming from? "Why would you want to marry me?" I asked, as I leaned forward. "Don't I have to be eighteen or something like that?"

Kelly twisted her lips upward. "I didn't say we were getting married tomorrow, I was just putting it out there," she said.

We both became quiet as the waiter approached with our food. I'm glad he did come. I didn't know what else to say to her concerning marriage. We both began attacking our food vigorously before the food was entirely on the table. I did so in hopes of not talking, and I think she dug into her food because she was hungry.

After a half hour of silence, it dawned on me where I knew that smell that I'd smelled at her apartment. It was a smell I would ingest each day while walking pass the crackheads outside my building on my way to work. It was a strong ammonia-like aroma that catches a person's nostrils immediately. I glanced up from my plate of food. Kelly's once radiant caramel skin had become a dull grayish color, as if she was losing her natural oils. Taking all this into account, I had to admit to myself that she was getting high.

I put my fork down. I stared at her as I sat back in my chair. She was acting like she hadn't eaten in days. Man, I know this wasn't happening to me! I asked myself. "I know you're getting high," I said.

I put it out there forcefully and with no hesitation.

Kelly stopped eating. She looked up from her plate and stared at me.

"Don't look at me like that," I said. "For the past two months, I've seen you hanging out with people I know indirectly from the street. These people who I know are into drugs. Either they're selling it or they're using it. Which one are you doing?"

"Why would you ask me that? What have I done that would make you question me about getting high? I'm your daughter's mother! How dare you ask me something like that, Anthony," Kelly snapped with pride.

I'd always had a knack about looking into people's eyes to see if they were telling the truth. When a person lies, they have a tendency to look away when answering your question or looking up as if in thought and finally attempt to convince you into what they were saying. Kelly did exactly that, and when she did, I knew she was lying.

"You know I don't do drugs, Anthony. You know my parents were drug addicts and how I grew up living from one relative to the next. Going to foster care and having no one there for me. I would never do drugs," Kelly said.

Her words were like syrup as they flowed from her mouth, I thought, as I continued to stare into her eyes. When she licked her lips and looked away, I knew she was lying. In the bottom of my stomach, I felt that pang of guilt. I can't explain it, but it was there.

I looked at the tip of her fingers on her right hand. They were brown with residue from smoking marijuana. I knew that because most of the boys I hung around smoked trees and all their smoking fingers resembled hers. She was lying. When I first met her, Kelly didn't smoke, but now she's sitting in front of me, attempting to convince me that she does not. Bullshit.

"I know you and my mother don't get along, but can I get Monique tomorrow?" I asked. "I want to take her to see my father."

"Of course, baby. That way I can have some free time to myself for a while to do woman things, or if you want, you and I can have the apartment to ourselves for a few hours," Kelly said. She took my hands into hers. "You're good for me, Anthony, and I'm good for you."

I nodded as I slowly slipped my hands out of hers and returned my attention to my food.

"I'm going to take you home tonight and make hot, passionate love to you, Anthony. You're much older in mind than you are in age, and that's what attracted me to you. I know people talk about our age difference, but if a person is happy, it doesn't make a difference what age they are."

I placed a piece of steak in my mouth as I stared at her in thought. What do you say to something like that? How do I express myself when she is thinking like this? If I were a hardboiled person with no feeling, I would've told her she was telling me madness and it wasn't at all sincere, but instead, I swallowed the steak and smiled.

I bounced Monique on my knee as everyone around shouted out, "Happy birthday" to her. It was her first birthday, and I was happy to be giving it to her. I glanced at my mother who was smiling at me. My thing with Kelly had come to a head about two weeks ago. I surprised her early in the morning. I walked into the apartment, and she was trying to block me from entering her bedroom as I headed toward the room to get my daughter. She had actually thrown her body between me and the closed door.

"What are you doing?" I ask her as she stood in front of me in her bathrobe. "I want to get Monique."

"Okay. Okay. I will get her for you," Kelly said. Her eyes were wide and desperate as she kept looking around while biting her bottom lip. "I had just changed her before you arrived and was putting her clothes on."

I looked at her. She smelled like she'd just gotten out of bed after having sex. I could smell it emanating from her. There was another smell as well. One that was distinctive.

"Stop playing and let me get my girl," I said as I tried to get around her. She placed a hand in the middle of my chest, stopping me. I took a step back as the reality of what was taking place dawned on me. "Do you have a man in there with my daughter?"

Her expression of shock was her answer. Her eyes gave her away as they blinked uncontrollably and then looked away.

"Bitch, you crossed the line!" I snapped as I literally picked her up by her waist and tossed her to the side. "What the hell are you doing in here?" I opened the door.

When the door swung open, I saw a man asleep in the bed. The man was knocked out. He was snoring so loud that he didn't even hear us on the other side of the door. My anger began to rise. When I glanced over to the right corner of the room and saw my daughter's crib, my anger exploded. She was standing up, holding on to the bars crying.

"Anthony, I'm sorry!" Kelly said.

I heard her, but my attention was for the safety of my daughter as I hurried across the room and grabbed her out of her crib. As I did, I heard some glass shatter under my foot. I looked down to see a crack pipe. I cursed as I lifted Monique out of her crib.

"Hey, man! What the hell is going on in here," the man said, as he sat up in the bed, looking around half asleep and half frightened. "This better not be a setup!"

I held my daughter tightly as I stared at Kelly. If my eyes could shoot lightning bolts, I would have struck her down. I glanced at the man. He must have seen the fire in my eyes because he was about to get out of bed, but stopped as our eyes met and slowly lowered himself back down.

"Anthony...I want to say—"

"There is nothing to say, Kelly," I hissed with maddening anger. My nose was flaring with increasing anger as I stared at her. An image of me walking up to her and slapping the shit out of her briefly passed through my mind, but I was raised better than that. "Words at this point are meaningless."

The woman standing in front of me, smelling like sex, had violated me to the very core of my existence. The mother of my child had disrespected me by bringing a man in the presence of my child to have sex, and she was getting high. She had taken my trust and threw it back in my face.

"I'm taking Monique with me. There's no way I will let my daughter be a part of your world at this stage in your life," I began. "You need to get some help or you will end up like your parents."

I made an attempt to exit the room by stepping around the broken crack pipe. As I neared the door, I grabbed Monique's baby bag. I didn't know what was in it, but it would have to do. The front closet held her heavy coats. I grabbed the nearest one.

Kelly stepped in front of me. We stared at each other for a fleeting three seconds.

"Don't belittle me by mentioning my parents, Anthony! And who the hell do you think you are by thinking I will let you leave with my child? So what? I might be getting high, but that doesn't stop me from being a mother. I can handle my responsibilities as to raising my child!"

"Hey, bro. She might be right in that regard. You know what they say. The woman can raise the girls and the men can raise the boys. Me, hell, I have two boys and they're mama is raising them. Momentarily though, until I get myself together," the man in the bed said.

I turned toward him. I shook my head as I stared at him. I felt the muscles in my arms tighten. "Man. You keep sexing her and let me raise my daughter," I said with heated venom I returned my attention to Kelly as he nodded his head. "First, she's not your daughter if you bring this man to your place to where your daughter lays her head. Secondly, your parents abandoned you as a child while they went out into the world and did their drug thing. You grew up feeling alone without them in your life. Do you think I will let that cycle continue with my own flesh and blood? Do you believe that I would let you keep my daughter knowing that you will eventually fall worse from using drugs? Nope. I would rather cut my own throat than let my daughter live with you. Now, you can either step aside peacefully, or I can knock you out of my way to get my daughter to safety. You decide."

We stared at each other. I could see anger building in Kelly's eyes. I watched as her lips curled up. I don't think it was the fact that I was taking my daughter. I think her guilt stemmed from me finding her in bed with another man. You see Kelly was a thinker of sorts. If she could manipulate a situation to her advantage by making you look like the culprit and feeling a sense of shame at the same time, then she was happy. At the moment though, I was holding the upper hand of morals, and she refused to submit to it.

"I will be coming to get my daughter," Kelly said as she stepped aside to let me pass. "Even if it means I have to go to court."

"Court? Hey, court involvement usually leads to paperwork being filed, which in turn leads to police inquiries and warrants are issued. Come on, people. We don't have to do that. Now I have to be a witness when called in by the court, and I can't do it, man. I have child support arrears and a few warrants from…well, you know where I'm going with this. Let's settle out of court," the man in the bed said.

I turned and looked at this person with contempt. "What's your name?" I asked him.

"There is no need to be taking names, bro. This was a one-night stand, and when you leave, I'm on my way out of here too. I was just trying to give a little input in a well-known situation in which men don't win in court when it comes to getting custody of their children. I tried it just last month when I contested my baby mama in having sole custody of my daughter."

"I thought you said you had two sons," I interrupted. "And what is your name? I mean, the way we're having this discussion, I feel you're part of the family in some freaky, messed-up way."

"Huh? Oh yeah. Well, people call me Glaze. My daughter is from my second baby mama. Anyway, I'm in family court about last year this time, contesting sole custody of my daughter. Her name is Chassity. She was five at the time." Glaze looked from Kelly to me. Seeing no response, he continued. "There we are standing in front of this white man who is about to decide what's best for my child. I interrupted before he could lay his judgment. I told him that I would voluntary forfeit my partition rather than have him rule against me."

"Glaze, I really need you to shut up right now, man," I said as I returned my attention back to Kelly. "If you want to go to court, it's cool with me, but remember, we're going to put it all on the table when we do go and especially when it comes to getting a drug test."

"Whoa! Whoa! Now you're crossing the line on that one, man," Glaze said as he sat up further in bed. "My baby mama, who has my sons, tried that one on me. I told her that if she tried to…"

"Shut the hell up, man!" I shouted. "This is between me and my daughter's mother. You got you a nut, now sit there and wait for another one." I looked at Kelly. "Don't make this something you won't like down the road. I'm not saying you can't come see our daughter. What I'm saying is that I will raise her."

Kelly walked to the end of the bed. She placed her arms over her chest and stared at me. "For now, you can do that," she said.

I held my daughter tighter as I nodded and walked out the room. I didn't look back because I had no reason to. There was nothing back there for me to see.

That had been then, and now, I didn't think much about it. The last I heard was that Kelly had lost the apartment for not paying rent. I had not seen her nor did I want to see her. For what? To bring up memories of a good thing gone bad. No, at the moment, sharing Monique's birthday with my family was all I was thinking about and the only thing that really mattered.

"Let me hold her," my sister Evelyn asked, as she walked over and took Monique out of my arms. "She's getting so fat and cute."

"Where is Ma?" I asked as I placed Monique in her arms.

"She's in the kitchen," Evelyn said while tickling Monique under her fat chin.

I stood and headed toward the kitchen. I hadn't really talked to my mother in a minute, and I needed to get her understanding of certain things.

When I walked into the kitchen, I saw my mother at the kitchen table, stirring something in a bowl. "Hey, Ma," I said as I walked over to the table. My mother could hit you with the meanest expression if she was upset. At the moment, she was upset.

"Anthony, tell me how are we going to care for that child? I go to college in the morning, and I tend bar at night. Your sister is in school, and you're working two jobs and going to school. Where will we find time to care for her?" my mother asked.

"Ma, I thought it all out. When we can't watch her, Kelly's aunt will. I've already talked to her about it and she lives in this building. Don't worry."

"Kelly? Does anyone know where she is at? Does she care about what's happening in her daughter's life? Horrible woman she is. She was a harlot if you ask me. What real woman molests a child at sixteen? What? Older men were just too much for her to handle."

I sat down. This was coming for a while, I thought, as I picked up a piece of fried chicken. I broke off the fatty part of the meat and began eating.

"There were many occasions in which I had to control myself from marching over to that woman's place and slapping the hell out of her for what she did to you."

"Ma, she didn't do anything I didn't want her to do," I said, as I bit down into another part of the chicken.

My mother stopped placing dumplings in the bowl. She glared at me. "So you think this is funny? I should reach across this table and slap the hell out of you. Go ahead and say something cute one more time."

I said nothing as I stared at my mother.

"What did your father say when you told him?"

I shrugged. "He laughed for a minute and then told me that it is tradition, son, in our Native American ancestry, that a man *must* provide and protect his family even if he must die in doing so. That there exists no reason why one cannot—period."

"Your father is a…what else did he say?" Ma asked.

"Anthony, you have entered a place that will eat at you from within. The stress of trying to do what's right for your child to the point of not knowing what to do with your child' and then accepting the fact that you're still a child yourself. It hurts me to my heart to have you live this way, but it is what it is and we have to grow from it. We will be fine in the long run, I know. It's the fact that we're simply here that makes me angry. I thought I raised you better than this. Where did I go wrong, son?"

"Who said you went wrong, Ma?" I said, as I touched her arm for reassurance. "I did what I did because I thought it was right in my own way of thinking. It had nothing to do with you. So I have a child of my own now, that doesn't reflect on how you raised me. What will reflect on how you raised me is how I will raise my own child. I love you."

I watched my mother wipe her eyes. A strong woman trying to stay stronger by not showing her weakness. That was my mother. She was a lioness in a jungle that could snatch up her cubs in a second and run into the jungle to protect them by forfeiting her own life if the need called for it.

My mother nodded. "With Tis gone, I sometimes feel that I could lose you at anytime as well, and that scares me to death, Anthony."

"I'm not going anywhere, Ma. You'll never lose me. As for Tis, it's not like we lost him altogether. It's just we have to go behind the wall to see him from time to time."

"It's wrong!" my mother snapped.

"It's a judicial system that doesn't show favor toward people of color, Ma, even when defending one's life. It's wrong, but it's been that way before we were even born, I guess." Now she did wipe away her tears. "I want you to be careful out there in those streets, Anthony. Do you hear me?"

"Yes," I said.

Entering the Gates of Hell

(Summer of 1987)

By the time 1987 rolled in, I was happy and enjoying my life. My daughter was four years old and she was talking. She was very bright and funny. There were times when she'd accidently rolled off the bed and then jumped up as if nothing happened, laughing hysterically. It was the summer time, and I had found myself a construction job in Brooklyn that was paying me twenty-five dollars an hour. I was part of an organization that concentrated on forming an alliance with developers who came into the minority community to build. State law required these developers to employ at least 20 percent of their work force from the residents of that given community. When we found this out, we formed a coalition that would look for these construction sites, and when we found them, that's when negotiations would take place. On many occasions, these builders would try to deny that such a law exists, try to use intimidation, or threaten to call the police. Of course, we were fully abreast of the law and its application as to how it applied to our actions.

When negotiations did not work, fifty young minorities with no jobs, no money, and mouths to feed came off the bus that we used to locate these sites and took over the construction site. Our modus: if we can't eat in our own neighborhood, we will not allow you to come here and eat (make money). Every minute there is no work, monies are lost, and we made sure that the work stoppage lasted at least a few hours. And we came back to the site every day until that foreman agreed that 20 percent of his work force would be men and women from that community. This was done on a daily basis, and on occasion, we would run in to the mafia who controlled the construction business in New York back then. However, our contact with these men were more business orientated; all they would always say is "I'm going to put ten of your guys to work on this project that will last no less than a year. You make sure that not another motherfucker comes through here and stop my job or all of you is outta here." And that we did; once our guys were working, that site would be protected from other coalitions coming doing the same. It was heaven in the hood for sure.

"Monique? Daddy's home," I said, as I entered our apartment. I headed to the living room and flopped down on the couch that was in front of the television. I'd worked hard that morning, and my body was tired.

"Daddy!"

I turned around to see my sweet, cherubim daughter come sprinting out of the room and leap into my arms. My sister had put on her a pink outfit that made her fat cheeks stand out.

"How's daddy's little girl?" I asked as I playfully bit her underneath her neck. "How was school?"

"School was so good today. I had to do finger painting and I used all of my colors," Monique gleefully said, as she giggled between breaths.

"And she made cupcakes today," a voice said behind me.

I looked up and saw Evelyn entering. She was wiping her hands with a towel.

"How many cupcakes did you make Daddy, baby?" I asked, as I put her down and watched her run to her aunt. "Did you make chocolate ones?"

"Yes," Monique shouted in joy. "I made six!"

"Six is good, baby," I said, as I stood up and stretched. "Daddy has to take a shower. Where's Ma, sis?"

"She was out on a date," Evelyn said.

I looked at her as I walked by, and my look wasn't a warm one. "What kind of date?" I asked.

"She's a woman. She can go out with a man if she wants to. Did you look like that when our father went out with women after he and Mommy separated?" I didn't say anything. "I didn't think so. She's our mother, but she's a woman, and like every woman, she needs the attention of a man if nothing more than a dinner and a movie, Shan."

"I hope that's all she's enjoying," I said with a grin.

"Shut up, silly!" Evelyn snapped. "Come on, let's go make some more cupcakes. Your father needs to get some rest."

Forty minutes later, I was sitting in the bathtub resting my body as the hot water soothed my sore muscles. The water felt good. The image of Monique skipping down the hallway behind my sister made me smile as I listened to her little feet. I closed my eyes and let the water drift me off into sleep.

Two weeks later, I was sitting in my girlfriend's house on Lenox Avenue. Her name was Sherry. She was a nice young lady that was very attentive to me. Like every young man looking for that right woman, Sherry appeared to be that woman for me. She could hold her own in the streets, and she was a woman who I respected, and the sex was great. It had been a while since I allowed myself to open up to a woman in light of my experience with Monique's mother. Sherry was more my age and we communicated better.

"Where are we going Friday?" Sherry asked. "I need to get out and get my dance on."

The thought of going out sounded good. I hadn't been out in a while and needed something different to do. I rarely went out anymore. With my job and Monique constantly needing attention, free time barely existed.

"Did you hear Chris got arrested?" Sherry asked me from the other room.

I was lying in bed, slowly dozing off. I sat up at the mention of Chris being arrested. He lived in my building, and we hung out from time to time. I'd been hearing rumors around Albany Projects of the police going on a fishing hunt for suspects and any information concerning a murder of a cab driver that had taken place in front of my building. Any information given leading to the arrest of the suspect(s), a one thousand dollars TIPS reward would be given. I had not paid much attention to this because it had nothing to do with me. This was not the first time I heard of someone being killed in this neighborhood.

Yet for the past two days, I was being approached by people informing me that the police had been inquiring about me and my whereabouts in relation to this murder. I was shocked when I found a detective business card under my door one morning. The words on the back of the card read: I would like to speak with you call me—Det. Fritzpatrick. I ignored it. Why would I be interested in talking to a detective? I had nothing to tell him and he had nothing I wanted to hear. But that was how detectives worked in my neighborhood. They told you anything to get you to drop your guard, then hit you in the head with something altogether different. Not to mention, just less than a year ago, the 77th Police Precinct was raided by the Feds for harboring a cesspool of corruption from armed robbery to drug sales. This was not a police station to trust, not at all. I use to see some of the cops come on the corner and take drug dealers' money and get back in their patrol car and pull off. They did not care. Now they want to talk to me—shit.

"Where did you hear that?" I asked with every bit of concern.

Sherry was coming out of the shower fifteen minutes later. A towel was loosely wrapped around her voluptuous body. She sat on the edge of the bed and began drying herself off with another towel she was carrying. "This can't be happening now, Shan. Our son needs you." At first it slipped by me, but then it hit me hard in the face. I turned to look at Sherry, and she was crying. We're going to have a son.

"Oh, one of my girlfriends said that she'd seen the police taking him out of his building in handcuffs. Rumor has it that he was one of the persons who were involved with the killing of a cab driver after robbing him," she said.

I was completely dumfounded of his arrest. Chris was not a neighborhood thug. The criminal act didn't coincide with the image I had of him. He didn't posses that kind of character to kill someone. Some people you can immediately pick up on their... how can I say this, demons. Their demons stood out no matter how hard they may have tried to camouflage them. Chris just was not the murdering kind of person to possess those demons, I thought.

"That's street bullshit!" I snapped. "Chris doesn't have it in him to kill anyone, Sherry—he just doesn't."

Sherry slowly turned toward me. There was a weird expression on her face. "The streets are saying that you were with him when he did it, Shan. They say it was a robbery gone wrong," she said.

It felt like Sherry had reached over and punched me in the stomach. My eyes became blurry, and I had to take a deep breath. I felt my hands shake. I was in shock.

"What...what did you say?" I asked her in a hoarse, controlled voice.

Sherry faced me. Her eyes where pleading. "Shan, I'm not judging you or accusing you. I'm just telling you what is being said in the streets around Albany Projects."

"Do you think I could take a person's life, Sherry?"

"No, I don't think you would ever do such a callous and reckless act against another human being, Shan, not you," she answered.

"I need to straighten this out," I said, as I stood up and began pacing the room. "How in the hell did my name get mixed up in this…madness?" I asked myself. I've never given anyone the impression that I was like that. Where was all this coming from? I must find out.

I continued doing what I always had done: going to work and caring for my daughter. The anticipation of having a son overwhelmed me in my thoughts. There were no visits from the police, and I was not hiding—for what. Chris was still locked up; he had been charged with felony murder in the death of that cab driver. The rumors were still circulating around the projects, but I paid them no mind because if the police were really looking for me, then why not just knock on my door. I still had not determined the origin of how my name got caught up in the mix and from who.

It was a warm day in June 1987, nearly three months after the killing of the cab driver that Sherry said that I needed to go talk to the police and get to the bottom of this before it gets worse. She came to me and gently hugged and kissed me. "I will be there for you, baby, no matter what. I love you." I decided to confront this matter head on. If the police would not come to me, I would go to them. I decided to talk to the fellows from the building to see what they had heard so I went downstairs, and in the lobby were Dale, Rick, Jazz, Shabazz, and Reggie and they were standing close together talking. As I approached, they all seemed to turn at once. "Hey, Shan," Reggie said. I immediately got to the point. "Have any police been in the neighborhood looking for me?" And that's when Dale said, "They just left. Two detectives just left the lobby and they asked us had we saw you," and it was then that I began to panic. The rumors were true, but I could not understand why. I have done no wrong. I must go to the police station and find out exactly why they are looking for me. What could they do to me?

I arrived at the 77th Precinct alone and within minutes was handcuffed to a radiator. I watched as police officers walked by me as if I were of no importance. Those that did acknowledge me did so with a disapproving stare. When I'd spoken to the detective working the case some time ago over the phone, he'd assured me that he was just following up on leads and was not accusing me of anything by asking me questions pertaining to the night of my whereabouts in regard to the murder. He'd assured me that if I came in and talk to him that everything would be worked out. Now, as I rubbed my chaffed wrist that the handcuff was connected to, I realized that it was a ruse to get me into the precinct.

As I sat on the hard bench, wondering where all of this was leading, I thought about my daughter. I asked myself if she'd eaten dinner and was okay. Like a concerned father, they were my priority. I looked up to see a detective with some papers in his hands coming toward me. I hope those were papers that told him they'd arrested the wrong person and were coming to let me go free.

"Anthony Faison. I'm Detective Fritzpatrick."

"How's it going, Detective Fritzpatrick? I've been here for a while now. I hope you're ready to take these handcuffs off so I can go home. I have to go to work tomorrow," I said, as I displayed a weak smile.

"Yes and no. The handcuffs will be coming off, but the part about you going home is no," Det. Fritzpatrick said. "I'm officially charging you with murder."

My mouth went dry. I blinked three or four times within a nanosecond at hearing the word *murder*. I said with difficulty, "You're charging me with murder?"

"Not just you. Your codefendant Chris Light is also being charged with the same crime," Det. Fritzpatrick said.

"My codefendant? What do you mean my codefendant?" I asked, as I flexed my handcuff wrist, unconsciously thinking I could will it to break.

"Well, the law defines *codefendant* as two or more individuals who have committed a crime together as just that," Det. Fritzpatrick replied.

"Codefendant?" I repeated as I watched Det. Fritzpatrick unlock my handcuffs. "I didn't even do this crime, so how can I have a codefendant for something that I did not do?" I watched his eyes. He glanced at me, and then averted them. "I don't understand what you're talking about. You're arresting the wrong man—I am innocent."

"Everyone is innocent when they're charged with a crime, Anthony," Det. Fritzpatrick began as he handcuffed me behind my back. "Your job and your lawyer's job is to prove the contrary. It's that simple. However, at this time, you're under arrest for murder."

Walking toward the back of the precinct where I would be held in the bullpen, I felt my feet grow heavy with each step. My legs became rubbery, and my vision blurred a little. Det. Fritzpatrick was half dragging me and half pulling me as he led me away. My mind had gone completely blank. What was I going to do? How did I get into a situation like this? I have always heard of men and woman being falsely accused and imprisoned, but not in a million years would I think that this would happen to me.

For some apparent reason, Det. Fritzpatrick came to the holding cell that I was in, handcuffed me again, and said, "Come on." His face seemed somewhat worried; I could not read him. He placed me in an unmarked car, and within an hour's time, we were in three different precincts in different parts of Brooklyn. Finally, after what seemed like eternity, we finally arrived at Brooklyn Central Booking where I was to be processed into the system. As Det. Fritpatrick walked away and left me detained with his partner, he looked at me as if he wanted to say something and then he spoke, "Make sure you get a good lawyer. Something is not right," and then he went silent.

Nineteen hours later and after bullpen to bullpen, I was at arraignment in Brooklyn Criminal Court. "The People of the State of New York against Anthony Faison, indictment number 5357/87," the judge says as he occasionally looks over his glasses at me. The judge goes on to say, "The defendant does not have an attorney, so the court will appoint one at this time." Since there were several attorneys sitting in court that usually accepts court-appointed representation, the judge assigned Ira Green to represent me. He was a man about seventy-five years of age, if not older. After a brief one-minute consultation with me, he states, "Not guilty, Your Honor. The defendant request bail at this time." The judge, once again looking over his glasses, looks down at me from the bench and says, "Bail set at one million dollars." I looked at my court-appointed lawyer and said, "Did he just say one million dollars?" His response was, "Yes, and that seems really high. Do you have a criminal record, Mr. Faison?" "No, I do not." Over my rambling thoughts, I heard the judge state, "Next court date, August 21 at 9:00 a.m., a little over two months from these proceedings." Right away, I knew that I was not going anywhere any time soon.

Two weeks later, I was standing in line to get lunch in the Brooklyn House of Detention located in the heart of Downtown Brooklyn. It had taken me that long to really understand my situation and recover from the shock of the entire ordeal thus far. As I evaluated my circumstances, I realized that I was in a freefall, and I was on a pendulum swinging back and forth. I'd found myself going to sleep at night with wild thoughts of me fighting every day or losing my mind to come to terms of what was happening to me. I did not have an answer for anything, and when I sought answers, I received nothing.

The first night that I arrived, I felt the humiliation of being violated. I had to strip naked, lift up my private parts, and afterward, I was told to bend over and spread 'em so that the officer can look between my ass to make sure I was not carrying any concealed contraband. Under different conditions and circumstances, that would have been a request for war. In jail or prison, it's a part of life. I sat in the cell and stared at the iron bars in front of me. Freedom, when taken from you, makes you evaluate everything in your life. I was sitting in jail for a crime that I had not committed. I was being accused of murder and robbery. The reality of that had nearly made me regurgitate.

The first week of my incarceration, my mother, sister, and Sherry had all come to visit me. I sat in the visiting room, staring at them. I think I was going through shock. There were hours as I sat in the cell, thinking of my situation. My mind became blank at times as I stared out in space.

"How can they charge you with murder?" my mother asked me.

"We're trying to get you a lawyer," Evelyn said, as she pleaded with her eyes for me to stay strong.

"How are they treating you in here?" Sherry asked.

From the tone of their voices, I could tell that they were more concerned about me than I was for myself. I watched my sister stare at me as if she was witnessing me lose my mind. Our eyes held each other's for a fleeting moment, then she smiled, which, in return, made me smile.

"I'm doing okay," I replied.

I sounded distant. I knew that. But I had a hard time focusing, and I was on the verge of a breakdown. Seeing the most important people of my life sitting there helpless, robbed of a son, brother, father, and friend without just cause. I tried to hide the sheer pain of not seeing my daughter, but my mother read me like a best seller. I often wondered how my daughter was handling my incarceration. My mother and sister refused to discuss it until now. "Mom," I said, "how is Monique?" She was quiet for what seemed like days and then she spoke with great pain. "Anthony, she cries every night. She jumps when someone knocks on the door, only to return in tears. She refuses to sleep until her daddy gets home. What are we to do, my son?" Mom asked. I felt like crying, I felt angry and I felt that I had to do all that I must to return to my family but how? I felt hopeless. For the first time in my life, I had no answer.

"I put one hundred dollars in you account to help you with the basic things while you're in here," my mom said, and it echoed in my ears as she looked around. "Some of these young boys look like children." She shook her head in disgust. "This is where they pile them up when they are at loss at what to do with them, I guess."

I listened to my mother, sister, and Sherry talk about what was going on out in the street with half an ear as I stealthily glanced around the visiting room. What was there to see? Young men like me caged in a modern-day slave den. Older men who could be my father or grandfather were engaged in the family connection with their loved ones. *How did I get here?* I asked myself for the thousandth time.

"Anthony! Anthony!"

I turned in the direction of my mother who wore an expression of concern as she stared at me.

"Yes!"

"I want to know if you want me to bring you anything next weekend," she asked, as she gently touched my hand.

I stared at her. I mean, I just didn't look at her at that moment. I took in the woman who gave birth to me, fed me, comforted me as a child when I was sick, and appreciated her caring, motherly demeanor. A woman who hugged me when I needed a hug and used the simple words of "I love you" during times of emotional strife in my youthful life, and then, right there at that moment, I understood the strength of a black woman, and it was mesmerizing to my mind. She was a woman who was simply more than that to a man who might one day ask her for her telephone number and her hand on a date, but she was, to me, my mother.

"No, Ma. I think…maybe you and sis should relax and let all this sink in," I said, as I took my son from Sherry and placed him on my lap. "This is a crazy place and I need time to…I guess to adjust to it."

"What? Um, Anthony—"

"Ma, I love you, but I'm in a different place right now, and seeing you makes it harder for me. I'm in here for murder! They are accusing me of taking a man's life! They are telling me that I could spend the next twenty-five years of my life in places like this, if not more. These feelings I'm going through are so strange. I want to scream some nights, and other nights, I want to grab a person—any person, by the throat and choke them. I want to get up and run to that exit door that you will be walking out. I want to take my son and never give him back. Ma, I'm caged in here like an animal in distress. And like any animal, I—"

"No, we're getting you a lawyer!" Evelyn snapped, as she reached over and grasped my hand. "We're a family, and if you are in jail, we're in there too."

I smiled. My sister had always been there for me. You could depend on her. Even though she was the younger one, she acted as if she were older than me. I nodded.

We sat there for an additional hour and a half when the booming voice of one of the CO's shattered everyone's family moment.

"Visiting hours are now over!"

Those words were the reality shocker that keeps a person grounded while doing time, I thought, as I looked into the innocent eyes of my son.

"Please begin heading toward the exits, people!"

Sherry and I stood up as I passed her Antwan. She grabbed me by my collar and kissed me hard on my lips. When she pulled away, she was crying.

"Shan, I will always be here for you. I love you too much to be without you in my life," Sherry said, as she turned around and headed toward the exit door.

My mother came up to me and gave me a hug and whispered in my ear, "Son, keep your faith and never give up hope," and then proceeded to follow Sherry out the door. Evelyn, my loving sister, I watched her approach. She was smiling.

Growing up, whenever I saw her smile, it seemed to take away some of my pain. At that moment as she drew near, I felt some emotional pain fall away.

"So, big brother," she began as she opened her arms toward me. "Give me a hug."

As I wrapped my arms around my sister, I felt a jolt of energy surge through my body as if she were giving me her strength. She whispered in my ear.

"I don't know what you are going through inside this place, Shan, but do not let it make you weak or forget how to stay strong and survive when times get difficult. You have to believe at all times and don't let any of this make you lose faith in yourself and in your plight," she said. "No one can fight this more than you can fight for yourself."

I pulled back from her and looked into her eyes. I could see the tears. I watched as she walked away with her head held high. *Another strong black woman*, I said to myself.

In the visiting room, we, the incarcerated, stood by our tables until all the visitors had exited, and then, we were ushered into the back and told to strip out of our gray jumpsuits that all inmates had to wear during visitation. Having to stand in front of any man and be made to lift my balls and turn around and bend over to show that I was not hiding contraband was humiliating and degrading.

As I walked back to the cell, I felt a presence slide up beside me. I glanced to the right of me and saw a small, caramel boy no older than seventeen beside me.

"Hey, what's up?" the seventeen-year-old asked me.

I was hesitant to respond, but not acknowledging him is being disrespectful in a way and that could lead to a confrontation.

"Hey," I said, as I continued to walk.

"My name is Chad. That was my family."

I nodded.

"I haven't seen you in the visiting room before. Did you just get here?" Chad asked as he came closer to me.

I felt myself tense. Why was this young man talking to me? What was there to gain in him having a conversation? Was he trying to feel me out? Was he trying to punk me or set me up? I had to let all these questions run their course. I have never been in jail before; therefore, I was suspicious of everything and everyone.

"That was my mother, sister, and baby mother," I said while giving Chad a quick glance.

"You from Brooklyn?" Chad asked.

"Uh-yeah," I replied.

"This is your first time, huh?" Chad asked.

I didn't want to answer the question.

"It's cool, man. This is my fourth time in this place. I've been doing time since I was twelve years old. Bouncing from foster care to youth incarceration facilities. They can change the name of a place, but it's all the same. Jail. I've been selling weed, coke, and dope. That's what I do. I sell shit, powerful shit. Right now, they said I made a sale to an undercover, but they're lying. First,

I do not do hand-to-hand sales. I get one of the young kids to do their thing for me. Every time I touch money, I switch it off to another runner. This way I never have any marked money or drugs on me. No sell money, no bust."

"That's…smart," I said.

I could say that I wasn't impressed with this young kid telling me how to conduct myself in the process of selling drugs, but I would be lying. He was no bigger than me, but he carried himself like he stood ten feet tall.

"Do you know how I came about that information?" Chad asked.

I stared at him as we continued to walk. This kid was something new on me; in his mind, he had been through a lot and had found an outlet to his grief in life by manipulating the system that had practically raised him.

"How?" I asked.

"When I was up in Farmsville, that's another juvenile lockup in upstate New York, my legal aid lawyer was a dick with a capital D. Every time I went to family court to protest them sending me back to my foster care mother, who use to beat the hell out of me, this idiot would say things like, 'You ought to be glad you have someone to go home to.' Or he'd say, 'A few slaps against the side of your head will make you have better character in life.' The old white bastard didn't know a fucking thing about foster care. Man, that woman used to throw me in a closet for three days with two slices of bread, a glass of water, and a pail for me to piss and shit in. She said she was punishing me for eating too much of the food that the foster care agency was giving her to take care of me. So in actuality, it was my money that I was eating up!"

I could see the anger exploding out of Chad as he told his story. There was probably more to his life than he was telling me, but I figured he was just giving me the lighter side of the story.

So one day, my lawyer comes to visit me. It was out of the blue, you know. He wanted to tell me that he had decided to give my case to someone more knowledgeable with cases like mine. Well, I thanked him for that because he wasn't going anywhere with the bullshit he was saying to me. It was a brief visit.

Going back to my dorm, I found four heavy-volume law books in my quad. I asked the CO who brought them, and he told me my lawyer did. The four books were CPLs.

"What is CPLs?" I asked.

"Criminal procedure law," Chad said, as he whipped some dirt off his new sneakers with a handkerchief.

We were nearing the cell block. "What do you do with books on criminal procedure law?" I asked, as the CO stopped in front of the cell that confined me and called for one of the other guards to open the gate. Chad began, "Learning how the law works keeps you from falling too far in the clutches, man," Chad replied with a smile. "If you know how the law can get you in jail, there are other laws that can show you how to get out. Go to the law library, Shan. Read how the legal system can shaft you or set you free. In any case, it will open your mind."

When the large metal gates closed and Chad and the CO began walking off, I was smiling. Chad a young boy who knew what most imprisoned men did not, had shown me a light, a light that was at that moment filling the darkness in my life. It was a light of hope. That night in the confinement of a prison cell, in the darkness of dark, I got on my knees and bowed my head and I prayed. I prayed so hard that I cried.

The Power of Knowledge

Any man caught in a situation where they feel they have been wrong constantly finds a way to right that wrong. It's that man's sole purpose to find that change, no matter what life throws at him; if he didn't, then his life would be one of pain and suffering. The day Chad and I had our conversation was the day that I began to fight. Some people fight with their mouths, fist, feet, or manipulation of other's emotions. I decided that words would be my sword of confrontation.

I followed Chad's advice about the law library the next day. I walked in the law library, thinking I knew what I was looking for. Fire was in my eyes as I hurried grabbing CPL books off the shelves, but my eagerness to find answers for my questions I hadn't asked yet would be slowed when an older brother stopped me after watching me for an hour jump from one book to another without any real definition as to what I was looking for. I was at the table reading when he approached me.

"No disrespect, young brother, but I've been watching you run around here like your head was chopped off. Do you mind if I ask you what you're looking for?"

I glanced up at the older man. He had to be in his early sixties. Again, suspicion took hold of me. Why was he concerned about my business? What did he want from me? That is always the question when living in jail. No one does anything unless they have an ulterior motive.

I shrugged as I returned my attention back to the book. "I'm just reading," I said.

"Young brother, you've been in here for hours now," the old man said, as he pulled back a chair and sat down. "Do you like real estate?"

"Real estate?" I repeated as I looked at him. "That can't help me in my situation. Why would you ask that?"

I watched him reach outward and touch the book I was reading. "That's the kind of law you've been reading for the past hour or so," he said, as he gently closed the book. "My name is Red. There is no need for me to explain to you why I'm called Red, is there?"

He was right. The man's light skin and red hair said it all. There were freckles all over his face. The name fit him perfectly. He had a protruding stomach that hid his belt, but he had a stern expression.

"So if you don't mind me asking, and I say this gingerly, young brother, are you in here for embezzlement or fraud?" Red asked.

That was the question that makes a man take a deep breath before answering. It was like I was in some confession booth whenever I heard someone ask the question.

"No, I'm in here for murder, but I didn't do it," I said quickly as I stared at Red.

"Murder, huh?" Red began as he tapped the book and stared at me. "Was it one of your rival gang members you did in, young blood?" he asked.

"What? I—"

"Forget it," Red said, as he waved his hand in front of his face like he was swatting flies. "It doesn't make a difference. Okay, if that is your charge, you need to be looking in CPL 125.25, which relates to the New York State murder statute and related case law. You must study this law before you can begin research, little brother. Law respects those who can show that there is an error.

It doesn't respect anyone who doesn't understand it. Do you get what I'm saying?"

I didn't. But I didn't want to tell him I was slow with the intake of the information, so I nodded.

"All right. You must search the law books, and you must be diligent in your research to show the court that you've been railroaded, misrepresented in a trial, or wrongfully convicted," Red said as he stood up. "I'm going to give you a couple of books that will guide you, but you will have to find your own way as to how you can beat your case. I can't teach you how to decipher law. You will have to get into that with your own mind. Lawyers aren't born, they are bred by the constant hours and years of learning the law. Remember that, young blood."

I watched Red walk away. I didn't understand everything he'd said, but I did understand when he told me that I have to find my own way as to what criminal law was all about. It was something entirely different for me. I was a little scared going into a world of words. I mean I wasn't an idiot when it came to being verbal to express myself.

"Listen, young blood," Red began as he dropped four books down on the table in front of me. "Law is the most confusing creation made by man in the use of words. You ever see those television shows where you have these lawyers standing in front of the judge pleading their cases?" I nodded that I had. "Now you have an image of how to stand tall when learning law. Don't expect your knowledge of law down the road will help your case, but it will build your confidence and not let you be deceived by the words of a court-appointed lawyer. Knowledge is freedom. Always remember that. I started doing time when I was fifteen years old. I have never had a man try to push himself on me while doing time because I presented myself with self-respect. I have been beaten by the police, COs, and bastards who thought they could take advantage of me. In the end, behind these miserable walls, all you have is your mental freedom and the fire to beat a system that was made to suppress a man, to break a man. If you stand up for what you believe in, then you've already begun the fight to confront those who think little of you. You dig what I'm saying, young blood?"

I was temporary in awe of this man who appeared out of nowhere to give me an understanding of what law was all about. He didn't have to give me the time of day, but he did. I watched him walk away. He didn't glance back. I felt a chill run down my spine as I reached for a book. It was heavy. I guess you can say heavy with knowledge as I opened the book and began to read.

Time passes slowly and at times very quickly when in jail. You have a lot of time on your hands when waking up thinking about freedom. You go to bed thinking about it. There were days when I would walk out of the cell and see a plain-looking female officer walking through making a count or checking cells. The longing for a woman during those times can be troublesome if a person succumbs to their sexual desires. I had to put these things aside.

Ten months would pass as I sat in Brooklyn's House of Detention. I'd gone back and forth to court for hearings during those months. I'd also learned a little about criminal law. Law is the most complicated thing written. I'd thought I'd have a case to present to my court-appointed lawyer whenever we had a court appearance, but the old guy would tell me that the case was either insignificant or didn't pertain to my case at all. Do you know how that made me feel? Thinking I was getting something done with my case and then have cold water thrown in my face. Some nights after going to court, I would sit in my cell and stare at the bars. My mind would be blank. How was I going to do this? Would I spend all my years sitting in prison? Can I survive in prison doing all that time? What will happen to my children? What about Sherry? Would she stand by my side after twenty years? So many questions. *Too many questions*, I thought.

My cot was a bed with a thin mattress, I stared at the ceiling. The names of previous occupants looked down on me. How long ago were those names written? I asked myself. I looked around my cell at other names written on the walls. It was a mausoleum of history of past criminals. I didn't see any logic in putting my name on a wall. I didn't want to be immortal on a wall of criminality.

I threw my feet out of bed and let them hit the floor hard. I ran my hands over my face. I was falling apart. I could feel it with every breath I inhaled. I was losing my drive because I was losing my direction toward freedom. Prison was beginning to drain me, sucking me dry with its stifling atmosphere. I was starting to lose that light that kept me driving toward it. I stood up and looked at my watch. It was three forty-four in the morning. I was anxious. I was becoming confused. I began pacing my cell like a wild man. I walked to the bars and grabbed them. I gripped them so hard I could feel my hands hurting. I pulled on them lightly, and then I began yanking them as if I could pull them out from sheer strength. I did that for ten minutes until I fell to my knees from exhaustion. I was hurting. I wanted to throw my body into the bars, hoping I could break them that way to get out. I wanted my freedom! I demanded my freedom!

I wanted to walk the streets again and not feel threatened for doing something I didn't do, and to do that, I had to let the world know that I wasn't a murderer. I didn't take a person's life. I can't run from something like this. No, I had to show the system that their attack against me would not go down in history as another black man taking another black man's life. I had to prove to everyone that I was innocent. I didn't want my family thinking I was a murderer. What about my mother? I know she didn't show it, but she was struggling to accept it. I was her son. I was accused of taking another man's life. That had to cause her pain.

I slowly stood up from the cold concrete floor. I leaned my head against the bars as I put my arms through them. I sighed with discontent. I realized that prison was a hard existence. It was a place of suffering and self-pity if you let it take hold of you. I couldn't let that feeling engulf me. If I gave up, I would be a memory of another young black male convicted of killing another black male. No. I wouldn't let that happen. I refused to let that happen. I would not become a statistic. I took a step back and breathed slowly. My head had cleared. My direction to survive in prison was magnified by my new realization that I was facing an uphill battle. A battle that was filled with obstacles that would either break me or make me better than I was. I walked to my bed and sat down as I reached for a CPL book that was on the floor. I had nothing but time on my hand, and I intended to use it…if it meant using it all, then that's what I would do to ensure I was proven innocent for a crime I didn't commit. If it took me the next twenty years to prove that, then that would be my eternal task.

The next morning, I was standing on line in the mess hall. Breakfast consisted of oatmeal, orange juice, toast, and powdered eggs. I had come to accept these meals like I'd come to accept standing in front of my cell bars waiting for them to open or watching the officers walk by my cell counting each morning, afternoon, and evening to make sure no one had escaped. I had no choice but to wait for my cell bars to open just like I had to wait until I was served my meal. With my tray filled with food, I headed for a table.

All of the tables were made of metal and were bolted to the floor as well as the metal round seats that were underneath them. The table I'd decided to sit down at was occupied by two other young men my age. I'd seen them on different occasions in the gym or passing each other during recreation time.

"What's up, Shan?"

I nodded in the direction of the dark-skinned young man who addressed me. His name was Danz. We used to talk when

I first arrived. He was from Hollis Queens, the place where I was born, and had told me that he was inside for burglary and attempted robbery. He was two years older than I was, but he acted younger than his age.

"Hey, man, breakfast is always surprising, right?"

I sat down next to the young man who'd just made the comment. His name was Justice. He was one of those cool dudes who laughed and smiled all the time, although he was facing thirty years in prison for two attempted murders and one kidnapping charge. How you can take that lightly, I didn't understand, but he did and I never once seen him have an attitude toward anything or anyone as he waited for his day in court.

I noticed Justice was wearing the latest pair of sneakers that had come out. Inside, everyone was allowed to wear their street clothes. The only time you were not allowed to wear them is when you went on a visit.

"What's up?" I said as I sipped some orange juice.

"It's quiet. Did you hear about my man Rockbody beating up a couple of COs last week?" Justice asked.

"Yeah, I heard, and I also heard how the riot squad beat hot blood out of his mentally challenged ass," Danz said and started laughing. "What fool tells a captain if he wants to have sex?"

"It's not the fact that he said what he said, it's the fact that he told the captain that and the captain is a man!" Justice said and hollered with laughter.

Man, I was in shock as I listened to them tell me the story. This was all new to me, and some of the things I was seeing and hearing were mind blowing.

"Isn't Rockbody that big muscled dude that we always see being escorted through the jail?" I asked. "The one that talks to himself?"

"Yep, that's him," Danz said. "Man, they say that they beat his ass so bad that blood was coming out of every hole on his body."

"They shouldn't have beat him like that. They knew he was on medication and possibly a 730," Justice added. "Bastard COs! Some of them are worse than these motherfuckers living behind these bars."

"You know what they say, Justice. The animals aren't the ones locked up, it's the ones carrying the damn keys to the cages!" Danz snapped.

"What I've come to realize since I've been coming in and out of these nuthouses is that no matter how civilized you try to act and be as respectful as you can, they're punks who bring out the worse in you, and when you snap and get to stabbing some of these knuckleheads up with a dull shank, then they want to send you to a psychiatrist, and then he wants to shoot you up with hallucinate drugs. I don't think that's right, you know?"

Danz and I both looked at Justice. The way he described the scenario, you would think he'd actually been through it himself, I thought.

"So, Justice," Danz said as he began twirling his plastic spoon. "Is there something you want to tell us?"

I looked at Justice expectantly. I arched my eyebrows while giving him a dubious stare.

Justice shrugged as he placed a spoonful of oatmeal in his mouth while stealthily glancing from Danz and myself. I felt a little tense for a moment as the three of us looked at each other and then all laughed.

Later that evening, I was in the law library. The months of eagerly learning law had impressed Red. He got me a job in the law library, working five hours a day. They paid twenty-eight dollars every two weeks, but I didn't care about the money, I wanted the experience that Red was teaching me, and no amount of money could compensate for that. He was a paralegal and knew what he was talking about. I grew to respect him for his legal knowledge.

I was placing some books in their right order on the shelves when I saw a man enter. He was an older man. His hair was completely white. He was a small man in height with smooth dark skin. He walked over to Red, and they began talking. I went back to placing books on the shelves.

"Shan?"

I turned toward Red. He waved me over.

"Shan can help you, Mr. Wilson," Red said.

They were sitting at a table. I climbed down the ladder and walked over to where they were sitting. I pulled out a chair and sat down across from Red.

"How can I help you, young man?"

Mr. Wilson laughed. "You're a funny, young man," he said, as he leaned forward on the table. "I have been charged with arson, but my lawyer is acting like he doesn't want me to beat this case."

"You need a new lawyer," I said.

"No, I need you to look at my case for me and tell me if my lawyer knows what he's doing or trying to drain me for my money. I will pay you one hundred dollars a week for two months. If my lawyer is doing right by me, then you made easy money, and if he's not, then you still made easy money…to a point. What do you say?" Mr. Wilson asked.

I looked at Red. He returned my stare and shrugged.

"Hey, young man, Red can vouch for me. I'm a man of my word," Mr. Wilson said.

I nodded. "Can I look at your indictment and other paperwork?" I asked.

"Sure. I will bring you all of my paperwork tomorrow," Mr. Wilson said as he stood up. "Red, thanks."

Red and I watched him exit.

I turned toward Red. "What was that all about?" I asked. I didn't want to get caught up in any trouble and especially with someone who commanded the awe Red was displaying toward Mr. Wilson.

"Mr. Wilson was once a powerful man in the late sixties, early seventies," Red began as he tossed his head in Mr. Wilson's direction. "There wasn't one ounce of heroin that didn't enter the five boroughs without his approval at one time. He was the biggest, unknown heroin distributor in New York, Chicago, Pennsylvania, Georgia, Detroit, and Miami. He never did one day in prison, and now, he is here for supposedly torching one of his clothing stores in Brooklyn. I guess there is still someone in the DA's office who remembers a man like that, and this is their chance to get him after forty years of him running the streets. He's legitimate now and rich. I hear he's very rich, and knowing someone like him can only help you if you need help one day."

I looked at Red. How can an old man like that be walking around in prison so wealthy? I asked myself. "Why isn't he in protective custody if he's holding like that? Better yet, why not make bail and fight it from the outside?"

Red smiled as he stood up. He looked down at me. "Young brother, a man like Mr. Wilson can walk around in any prison in New York, and no one will even think about touching him or exhorting him. He's walked with real gangsters in his day that makes these young wannabe gangsters in here step aside when they see him walking toward them. I've been doing bids for a long time. I know who the punks are and who the undercover bitches are, walking around here thinking they're men, but under all that muscle, they're women pretending to be men. Hoes with flaps between their legs to protect the dust from getting into their ass. Hopefully, Shan, you can beat this murder charge and get back into the streets and live a good life, but right now, at this moment, this is your life. You know how to point out your enemies by the way a man carries himself in here. I or no one else will be able to teach you that lesson. You will have to feel it in your gut, your very essence to survive in this cesspool that was created to imprison men and women. I can teach you law, but only you can teach yourself how to survive behind bars.

"You surround yourself with men who are men. Not little boys trying to be men by the fact that they tell you stories of how they were running around in the street. How much money they were making selling drugs, doing robberies, or any other form of making that dollar. Fuck them! When you think you've made a friend in here, and when you need him and he doesn't come through, what have you made?"

I was perplexed by the conversation I was having with Red. Out of all the months that were shared legal scenarios, I'd never known him to speak so vigorously. It was like he had a lot on his mind and the sight of Mr. Wilson had brought it to a head. I was hesitant to answer the question as Red stood there, staring down at me.

"Uh, I guess it shows that trust have to be really limited as to who you give it to?" I said without much conviction.

"Man, you are young and naïve! And for that, I will excuse your innocence of the facts around you. Most of these idiots in prison are here because they want to be here. They never took the opportunity to see their real lives for what they were and how they could improve on their lives. A psychologist would diagnose a man like me as being antisocial. A person who cared about nothing or no one. I've lived my life the way I walked it. I have no kids. No woman to come see me or for me to worry if she's in the street sleeping with someone I know. I'm that kind of man who doesn't give out trust easily because I've been betrayed for most of my young and adult life. In here, you'll be conscious of every person you come in contact with because a person will smile in your face and tell you how much you two are cool, and when you least expect it, motherfucker will stab you in the back. I liked you the moment you walked in here that day trying to pull your life out from under the rock the judicial system has laid on your back. If I didn't, I would've sent your young ass out of here or ignored you altogether. Trust in prison is a priority and it's a rarity. You can meet good dudes in here, and you can meet snakes with venomous fangs. Know the difference, young brother. Mr. Wilson is a good man. Treat him right. Don't try to pick him like a grape off a vine, and he will return your generosity tenfold. I have respect for you because you know what you have to do to turn this madness around that's placed you in here, but everything I've told you are things I'd never reveal to anyone else, so that is trust, Shan. Keep that close to your heart when you run into someone that seems real in this shallow-ass world called prison!"

I simply nodded in agreement. I had no words after that diatribe. Red always seemed like a quiet thinker to me, but after hearing him speak, I realized that he was a man who had his own demons close by, and at this time and day, he wanted me to hear his pain.

"Good," Red said. "Do right by Mr. Wilson and he will take care of you."

Red was right about Mr. Wilson. I helped him with his case for six months. They'd denied him bail due to his past history of police contact over the years, but most of that contact came from him being young and was nearly thirty-five years ago. Although he was paying a private lawyer he'd obtained in which he paid the man fifteen hundred dollars each court appointment, the man wasn't worth ten cents. He worked out of his office on Park Avenue, but writing a motion for Mr. Wilson's case was like him trying to write an essay. The man couldn't put it together effectively. So I took over writing Articles 78 for Mr. Wilson and writing discovery motions. Most of the motions I'd written for Mr. Wilson were upheld. I asked the court to acknowledge a motion for a bail hearing. It was granted two months later.

I was sitting in my cell one late evening after coming from the law library. My eyes were tired from all the reading of law books. I saw a shadow fall over the little bit of light that was shining through my bars. I was eating a piece of carrot cake when I looked up.

"Hey, Shan," Mr. Wilson said, as he stood in front of my cell wearing a nice blue suit. "I'm about to hit those concrete streets again."

I walked to the bars. I stuck my hand through them. "I'm glad you're getting out, Mr. Wilson," I said.

"I'm getting out because you knew how to work that legal jargon to get me bail. I still have to go to court, but it's better to go from the street than from inside," Mr. Wilson said, as he shook my hand. "You're a good, young man. I will keep you in my prayers."

"You take care of yourself out there, Mr. Wilson. It was good knowing you," I said.

"Listen, I heard about your case and…well, I will be checking on you to make sure you're okay from time to time. A man like me likes to stay in the shadows. You know what I'm saying."

I didn't know what he was talking about, but I refused to let him know that.

"Shan, thanks," Mr. Wilson said as he turned around to leave.

I watched him walk away. His back was straight and his head was held high, the smell of freedom made your back and shoulders stand out when you knew you were going to be seeing it, I thought, as I continued watching him take long strides down the corridor. I smiled as I walked back to the cot and sat down while picking up one of the many law books I had in the cell on the floor. I opened it with a smile. It felt wonderful to see someone going home.

Four months later, I was transferred to Rikers Island. It was spring of 1988.

Rikers Island could be defined as an island of the most feared, ruthless, debased men ever to walk the streets of New York City.

I was twenty-one years old now. My son had turned one and I'd missed his first birthday. His mother had sent me pictures of the party she'd given him, and those pictures made me smile. Antwan looked funny with cake all over his face. I tried to decipher who he resembled as I stared at his picture for over an hour. I couldn't. His features were still coming into their own. I didn't know if he looked like his mother. Yet his picture kept me smiling all day.

Rikers Island is different from Brooklyn House of Detention. There seemed to be more of a hostile environment within its walls. When I say that, I am referring to all the boroughs being placed in one hole, and that hole opening up every now and then to let off steam. Steam that usually results in whole-scale rioting. Yet changing the culture of it wouldn't work. Rikers Island was a hell that festered with each passing day.

It was warm outside as I walked the yard the next day. I liked the brown grass under my feet and a bright sun above me. It gave me time to think about my case, my children, my sister, my mother, and my brother, who, at that time, was doing twenty-five years in prison for simply defending himself. I didn't know what to think concerning Sherry. She was a beautiful young woman, and I knew there were men out there trying to get with her and eventually one day will. That fact had me angry at times, but what could I do? What could I say? Every time she visited me, she told me she loved me and that she would be there for me no matter how long I was inside, but I had my doubts concerning the truth of those words she'd constantly whisper in my ear as we sat across from each other and would stare into each other's eyes, wishing things were different. The reality of that was she could walk away from me at any moment, and there was nothing I could do or say about it to prevent it from happening. I was in prison and would be in here for some time if I couldn't get someone to believe me. Someone to reinvestigate the circumstances that lead to the victim getting shot and find the real killers. That's what I need.

A crack user by the name of Carolyn Van Buren had placed me and Chris Light in the back of a cab and said she'd seen me shoot the cab driver from two blocks away, at night, in the wee hours of the morning. Unless she possessed superhuman eye vision, I couldn't understand how the police and the DA office could accept her testimony as true.

As I learned how to request documents pertaining to my case, I began seeking all witnesses and evidence the police had gathered against me, and that one witness was all they had. A witness that admitted to smoking crack and drinking the night she alleged to have seen me shoot a man. I walked the yard with my fist balled up deeply in my pocket as I grew angry at the thought of this woman, this deplorable person saying that she'd seen me kill someone. Man, I wanted to run toward the ten-foot fence in front of me and climb up over it as I ran for freedom. But how far would I get before being shot down only to have the truth die with me? Why should I have to even think of running for something that I know I have not done? No, I will never run—I will fight.

I have come to realize the confinement of prison. It is a horrible place for a person to live. It is an arena of men who deem themselves to be beyond the laws of the common man; they are the men who want everything in life that is good but don't want to put in the moral work to get that goodness. Hustlers, thieves, murderers, rapist, extortionist, kidnappers, child abusers, bank robbers, gangbangers, wife beaters, and contract killers were all placed in a boiling pot filled with time.

These men sit around preying on each other's vulnerability. I had come to truly see the world I was living in with each passing day, and that world was getting greyer before my young eyes. It was a breeding ground for those whose skills were little, if none, when it came to doing crimes, but by the time they'd graduate from prison, they would be master criminals.

𝕿eeth of the 𝕭east

(Spring 1987)

It was the beginning of fall of that year when my codefendant, Chris, and I, began choosing our jury to begin trial. I'd never done anything like picking a jury before and it was all new to me. The ADA who was supposed to represent the people of New York gets to pick what jurors he thinks will lead to a conviction. And the defense, which consists of Chris, myself, and our defense attorneys, would attempt to pick jurors that we feel would be fair and impartial. It's like throwing a set of crap dice on a ragged velvet table with lumps on it. The dice can bounce from snake eyes to a marvelous seven on the first roll. You don't know what they are until the dice stop spinning. Then all you have is prayer!

"We are sitting in this court room today to bring justice for a man who was trying to provide a loving home for his family by working twelve hours a day, six days a week, driving a cab in a difficult place like New York City. A hardworking individual that wanted the success of the American dream. That dream was cut short with the horrific act of murder inflicted on him by the two defendants sitting to the right of me. Anthony Faison and Chris Light!" snapped ADA Peter Bronski.

I was sitting at the defendant's table with my court-appointed lawyer, Ira Green, and Chris was sitting to the left of me with his lawyer. I felt violated as I watched the ADA prance around with his gray Brooks Brothers suit on and his black shoes. A courtroom I came to realize was a room of performances. Lawyers are legal actors trying to convince the jurors to see their point of legal argument, no matter how humiliating or false that it may seem as long as their theatrics brought a conviction or acquittal. They rarely care about the truth. They cared about winning and improving their ratio that would look impressive on their resume when they applied for some other position to further their legal careers.

"In our society, we try to award those that stay within the spectra of our laws by encouraging them to teach their children to follow with positivity in their footsteps," Peter Bronski began. "Yet as we sit here today, the victim of this hideous crime can't tell his children to follow in his footsteps of positivity because his life was cut short by the senseless act of the two defendants before the court at present. I will prove to you without a shadow of doubt that these two defendants murdered the victim in cold blood for the sole purpose of robbing him."

I leaned toward my lawyer, Ira Green. I whispered in his ear. "Can he act that way in picking the jury?" I asked.

Ira Green turned toward me, wearing a frown.

"Anthony, this is how a jury gets picked. The jury is being sung to sleep in hopes of getting a conviction. Don't worry, we will have our say today as well. I've been picking juries for over forty years. These gray hairs on my head didn't come from playing golf, but from finding the right presentation in my oral rebuttals when the time came. So relax and take comfort in what a trial is all about," he said. "I'm sixty-nine years of age, and with age comes knowledge and patience. Trust me. We will be fine."

He patted me on my shoulder reassuringly as I went back to writing in my yellow legal pad that was in front of me. I glanced over at Chris and saw him writing in his legal pad as well. Taking notes during trial and the hearings gave me the chance to go over things once the day was complete. It also ensured me that I could find contradictions in the course of the trial sometime down the road if I needed it.

"Ladies and gentlemen, I will expect nothing more of you than a fair conviction in which you can go home after this trial and say that you delivered justice to a just cause. Thank you," said Peter Bronski as he spun around on the heels of his shiny black shoes and walked back to his table.

"Mr. Green, are you ready for your presentation?" Judge Kreindler asked as he looked down.

My lawyer stood up and walked around the table to stand in front of the jury. I noticed that his suit was wrinkled and probably hadn't been pressed in weeks. I shook my head. Appearance means a lot, I admitted. I, on the other hand, was wearing a nice blue suit my family had brought me a few days ago along with two more suits. I know it probably set my mother back a good penny, and I begged her not to buy them, but that was my mother's way of being in my corner. I turned around to see who was sitting in the courtroom. I saw my mother, sister, and Sherry. They all smiled at me. I smiled back. Returning my attention back to my lawyer, I wished he'd worn a better suit.

"Jury, I may not have the flash and youth as my esteemed colleague, Mr. Bronski, but I will present you with the truth, and the truth is that my client, Anthony Faison, did not commit this horrific crime. He is a young man who has never been in trouble before these accusations were brought against him. And that's what they are, accusations nothing more. He is innocent until proven guilty.

"Your concentration of this trial will bring justice in its natural habitat for this man. Thank you," Mr. Green said.

I sat back in my chair with my mouth open in shock as I watched my lawyer return to the defense table. His one-paragraph outline was all the jury received. I leaned into his shoulder when he'd sat down.

"Is that it?" I asked. "What happened to a little more force and persuasion?" I asked.

Ira Green patted the back of my hand. "Anthony, this is going to be a piece of cake to beat. Relax. Trust me," he said.

I took a deep breath as I gingerly slid my hand from under his. He was a man with forty-five years of experience, I thought. He knows what he is doing. I hope. Man, do I hope he does because my life was on the line.

I watched as Chris's lawyer stood in front of the jury and presented his client position. I had to admit, Chris's lawyer was just as good as the ADA Peter Bronski. It probably had to do with the fact that Chris's family had retained him a private lawyer and not a court-appointed one like mine. For most of the day and for the next three days, we picked a jury.

I was sitting in the law library reading on a case when I saw CO Watson approach. "Hey, Faison, I see you on the court calendar for trial all week," Watson said. He was standing in front of me. "Not to be prying in your business but I hear how you're telling anyone who will listen that you did not do the crime you're accused of. I don't judge anyone. I simply make sure that they are locked up nice and tight when my shift is over. I said that to say this. I have seen a lot of men walk through these halls saying they didn't do a crime, and when they start trial they take a cop-out that was offered to them early on. Is that going to be your walk down that road when it looks like things aren't going your way?"

I didn't know where this approach had come from. I spoke to CO Watson from time to time, but not to the level where he could pin a cop-out on me like that. I was surprised. I leaned back in my chair and crossed my arms over my chest as I looked up at him.

"No disrespect, CO Watson, but I didn't do this crime, nor did my codefendant. I'm in here because…I don't know. I guess someone felt it was joke time on Anthony Faison, but you can believe your pension that I will never cop-out to something I didn't do. I would go to hell and fight three pit bulls before I tell a judge in my own words that I committed this crime. I'm innocent and will continue telling anyone who'd listen that I did not kill anyone for money or anything else. I picked a jury. I will let my choice in that jury tell the world my story, but I'd be damned if I tell someone something that isn't true."

My words were firm. My voice was hard with belief in myself. I meant every word that came out of my mouth, and I guess CO Watson felt my seriousness because he smiled as he nodded and walked away without saying a word.

I was sitting in the visiting room the next day after that conversation with CO Watson, watching my mother, sister, daughter Monique, and Sherry with my son approach. It was good to see my daughter.

"Hello, family, "I said as everyone sat down.

"Hi, Daddy," Monique said.

"Hello, my baby," I said with so much excitement. I was happy and sad at the same time as I smiled at my lovely daughter. She was growing into a lovely girl. In my heart, I knew that she, being a girl, my presence in her life was essential. Without that male dominant figure in her life, I was afraid that she may some day feel the need to find an illusionary father image in the street. He would be an imaginary figure that would exploit and take advantage of her. The thought of this happening due to my lack of presence saddened my heart. Every man feels a need to protect their daughters from those who prey on the vulnerable, namely children. They are predators of young girls' flesh when their minds are innocent and their bodies are ripe and adult looking. I see them in the jail and I encounter their actual cases in the law books. I would have to guide my child from behind bars. That would be a task filled with struggles, I knew that, but what else could I do?

"Anthony, how does it look for you when trial starts next week?"

"That's a good question, Ma, because I don't know. They say they have one witness. My lawyer submitted a discovery motion that compels the ADA to disclose all the evidence that they have, including witnesses, and supposedly, she lives nearby," I answered.

Sherry handed me my son.

"I could ask around about her," Evelyn said.

I shook my head. "No, that would be witness tampering, and it would look bad on me if the prosecutor found out. No, I will work things out from in here. Thanks, sis. I appreciate the effort," I said, as I tickled my boy's fat stomach. "He's getting big."

"Uh-huh and he misses his father," Sherry said, as she laid her hand on my thigh.

Man, I hadn't been with a woman in over a year. Her touch was so comforting to me. As a man denied a woman for so long, we pick up on every particle of a woman once we get close to them. I could smell the perfume reeking off her sexy body, and my heart went racing with excitement. The blouse she was wearing was specifically for me because it left little to my imagination as I watched Sherry move in it. Her breasts were enticing, and I tried not to stare at them too long because of my mother and sister's presence, but Sherry would catch me from time to time and smile at me.

"I was thinking about our conversation two days ago, Anthony. I've been scraping up some money to try and get you a private lawyer."

"Ma, I know I sounded upset when we had that conversation, but don't put yourself in debt trying to make something happen for me," I said. "I will make do with what I have. I know a little about the law now, so I'm not that much in the dark when it comes to filing motions on my behalf."

"Well, maybe so, but I'm going to look into a few of them anyway. Not hire anyone, but just inquire," she said.

That was my mother. She was a woman of determination.

I smiled as we talked of other things besides court to pass the time, and it was good time in passing in the presence of my family. Before we knew it, visiting hours were over, and I was saying good-bye to my family.

The days went by quickly. My trial day came quicker than I expected it. I was sitting at the defense table on a Monday morning, watching Judge Kreindler give the rules of law concerning the crime I was accused of, what the jury could and could not do pertaining to the law, and how it relates to my particular criminal charges. It was all the typical diatribe that came with the preparation of a trial.

"What do you think our chances are, Mr. Green?" I asked my lawyer, as he sat writing furiously on a yellow legal pad. "I think the jury looks even," he said.

"Anthony," Mr. Green said as he looked up from the pad. "Law is the bastard of civilization. It takes one moment to catch you up in its rapture only to spit you out viciously when it's being disputed by another case saying the opposite of your representation of a motion. In other words, son, it's a tossup that can go either way."

I had to look at him. Was he saying I can beat the case or was I going to get convicted? *Hell, a simple yes or no would've sufficed*, I thought.

Judge Kreindler began, "I will not tolerate any grandstanding by any counsel in my courtroom, and when I make a decision, it is not to be questioned then and there. If you feel your client's rights have been violated at any time during these proceedings, I recommend that you object to preserve your issue on the record or request a sidebar—understand? Other than that, respect my courtroom."

"Yes, Your Honor," both defense attorneys said in unison. However, the ADA Bronski did not respond. I found this to be unusual. Was Judge Kreindler's instructions meant to silence the defense?

"Mr. Bronski, I believe you have the opening floor," Judge Kreindler said. Call your first witness."

I noticed that Peter Bronski was wearing a new suit. A black two-piece suit with a light gray shirt, black tie, and shoes. I could say this about the man: he stood out meticulously in front of the jury for sure. I glanced over at Chris and I could see his expression was as intense as my thoughts about the trial.

"I will prove today that these two defendants committed the crime they're being accused of with no prejudice whatsoever," Peter Bronski said, as he walked to the middle of the courtroom floor. Crossing his arms over his chest, he spread his legs as he smiled at me. *He was a vicious man*, I thought, as I gave him a hard stare. I could tell by his arrogant demeanor he was a man who was used to getting what he wanted. "The witness I am about to call to the stand will place Mr. Anthony Faison and Mr. Chris Light at the scene of the crime. She will tell you what she saw on the night in question. I would like to call to the stand, Ms. Carolyn Van Buren."

I sat there for a moment, refusing to look at this person entering the courtroom and walking toward the witness stand. Then I looked up; she was wearing a pants suit that clearly was too big for her. I could tell that she was a woman of questionable standards by the way she carried herself. I'd never seen her before that day and wondered what would make her lie on me. I had no answer as I watched her get comfortable on the witness stand.

"Would you please state your name and address for the record, ma'am," ADA Bronski asked.

"Uh…my name is Carolyn Van Buren and I live at 1400 Bergan Street, Brooklyn, New York," Carolyn said nervously.

"How long have you lived at that address?" Bronski asked.

"All my life."

"What kind of work do you do, Ms. Van Buren?"

"I…aint got no job," she said, her voice trembled as she glanced at the jury.

"That is understandable. Our economy is in a downward spiral and your situation is not uncommon. Ms. Van Buren, may I call you Carolyn?" Carolyn Van Buren nodded that he could. "The two gentlemen sitting at the table behind me, do you recognize either of them?"

Carolyn nodded.

"Ms. Van Buren, we need to hear your response when asked," Judge Kreindler said.

"Do you recognize either man sitting at the defense table?" ADA Bronski, asked again.

"Yes, I recognized both of them," Carolyn said.

"Have you seen them…around in the neighborhood where you live?" Mr. Bronski asked.

"Your Honor, I object!" Attorney Green said as he leaped up out his chair. "The prosecutor is leading the witness."

"Sustain. Mr. Bronski, let's stay on course with your questioning," Judge Kreindler said.

"I apologize, Your Honor. Let me rephrase my question. Ms. Van Buren, have you ever seen these two men before today?"

"Yes, I've seen them around the neighborhood where I live," Carolyn said as she fidgeted with what was left of her fingernails. "I know Shandoo and Chris."

"Shandoo and Chris? Which is which, Carolyn?" Peter asked.

"Shandoo is the little one and Chris is the big heavyset one," Carolyn said.

"Let the record show that the witness described Anthony Faison as 'Shandoo' and Chris Light as 'Chris.' The defendants currently sitting at the defense table. Go on, Carolyn. Do you know anything else concerning these two men?"

"I object, Your Honor, Counsel is leading the witness again," Mr. Green said, infused with obvious anger.

"Overruled, Counselor. The witness is merely answering the question,"

Judge Kreindler said. "Continue answering the question, Ms. Van Buren."

"I heard that Shan—"

"Anthony Faison is the person you're referring to, right?" Peter cut in.

"Yes, Anthony. Well, in Albany Projects, he was going around saying that he knew something about the cab driver being killed," Carolyn said.

Defense Attorney Green, though up in age, nearly knocked the table over as he leaped out of his chair. "I object to this line of questioning by the people, Your Honor! This is hearsay! ADA Bronski cannot produce before this court any evidence to prove that my client said anything to anybody. This is clearly hearsay," he snapped.

"The question is part of the answer as to how Ms. Van Buren knows the defendants, Mr. Green. The people have established that she's seen them in her neighborhood. That being confirmed, I will overrule the defense and allow the questioning to continue," Judge Kreindler said. "Please go on, Ms. Van Buren."

"That's what was being said around the block," Carolyn said.

I'd been writing with unbelievable effort as I sat next to my lawyer, slightly shaking my head. I'd write something and pass the note to my lawyer who would read it, then shake his head in either a "no" from side to side or a "yes" with his head going up and down. I'd never seen Carolyn Van Buren before in my life, even though she testified to living in my community. So how could she say she knew me or that I'd made such a comment.

"Ms. Van Buren, did you witness a crime on March 14, 1987? A crime that has brought theses two defendants before this court," Peter asked.

"You mean the night the cab driver was killed on Albany Avenue?" Carolyn asked.

"Yes, Carolyn. Tell us in your own words what you saw on that night," Peter said, as he walked across the floor with his hand behind his back.

I noticed that Carolyn Van Buren kept looking at Peter Bronski with some tense expectancy. Carolyn was cautiously weighing each word that came out of her mouth. I would find out much later why she was acting that way.

"Well, it had to be about four-thirty in the morning. I was going to the store," Carolyn began. "I turned the corner and saw a cab parked near Albany Avenue. I heard a gunshot, and when I looked in the direction of where it came from, I saw Sha—I mean Anthony Faison, standing by the front driver side with a gun pointed at the cab driver. I also saw Spa—I mean Chris Light getting out of the other side. They looked around and started running away from the cab toward St. Marks. I stood there for about ten minutes and then I walked away."

"Are you sure that you'd seen the defendants getting out of the cab on that night in question?" Peter asked as he walked toward the jury. "What makes you so sure that the persons you saw exiting that cab were Anthony Faison and Chris Light?"

"Yes, I'm sure," Carolyn replied.

"That's bullshit!"

I turned to the sound of the voice and saw that it was Chris. He was standing up with his fist balled on the table as he stared at Carolyn Van Buren. His lawyer was trying to get him to sit back down.

"Mr. Light, those outburst will not be tolerated in my court!" Judge Kreindler snapped, as he slammed down his hammer. "I suggest you sit down before I have you escorted back to the holding cells and you will be watching your own trial on a circuit TV."

I watched as Chris's lawyer slowly pulled him back down into his chair. I knew what Chris was going through as I listened to Carolyn Van Buren tell one lie after another, and there was nothing I could do. I felt violated by her act of blatant deception. It felt as if my skin was slowly being pulled apart from my body.

"All right, we will take lunch and will return at two o'clock," Judge Kreindler said, as he slammed down his hammer. "When we return, I hope everyone is a little calmer."

Everyone stood up as the judge exited the courtroom. I watched as a court officer came over and escorted me toward the back where the holding cells were kept. Chris followed me with two escorts of his own.

Twenty minutes later, Chris and I was sitting in the bullpen. I watched Chris pace back and forth like a ranging bull, as his nose flared open and close. Yes, I knew this to be a painful reality. One witness, no fingerprints, no DNA, no physical evidence, and we were sitting at a trial. I couldn't believe it. How did it get this far with that kind of evidence?

"Man, this is some real bullshit," Chris began, as he glanced from me to the bars. "Hey, Shan, I'm not feeling the way this case is proceeding. Peter Bronski is a vicious bastard. He dresses sharp and uses his sharp wit to make us look bad. He knows this is all bogus."

I pressed my lips together as I extended my crossed legs outward while placing my hands behind my head.

"Have you ever seen Van Buren before?" Chris asked

"No," I said. I stared at Chris. Contemplating my next comment, I had to make sure Chris knew where I was coming from. "Hey, you can't be blowing up like that in court, Chris. You have to be cool, man. The way you act will certainly influence the jury when they're in session, rendering their verdict. We both know that we did not commit this crime, and the jury has to see it as well. We have to keep calm." "Okay," Chris said.

Chris looked at me. "I don't see why you're acting so cool."

I shook my head. "I have some faith in the criminal justice system and jurors of my peers. I know they're not going to come back with a guilty verdict on us. The reality of this whole thing is phony to me. No person in their right mind is going to convict us on the flimsy evidence that the district attorney is presenting. So yeah, I'm not worried," I said.

Was I? Was I telling myself this to keep my own anger bottled up, or was I really convinced they wouldn't convict us on trumped-up charges. "So what? We sit there and listen to Van Buren accuse us of killing this man?" Chris asked as he went and sat back down.

"Yep, that's exactly what we do," I said.

Chris leaned his head against the wall and stared at the ceiling. "This is bullshit," he said.

An hour and a half later, we were back in the courtroom. Chris's lawyer was now questioning Van Buren. I was impressed by his questioning tactics and how he made her feel flustered whenever she tried to evade the question of her using drugs. Chris's lawyer was well worth the money his family was paying for legal representation. The man was powerful in his directness.

I was feeling the tide turning in our favor as I watched Chris's lawyer corner Van Buren in her discrepancy about why she'd come forth to implicate us. As I placed my elbows on the table, I heard a strange sound. The voice of Chris's lawyer was a baritone of force. Yet what was that sound? My ears had pricked as it continued. It was coming from the right of me. I turned. Sitting there with his eyes closed and his chest rising and falling in rhythm was my lawyer, Ira Green. The man was sleeping. Sleeping! What the fuck! I couldn't believe what I was seeing. My life was on the line, and this man, a man who'd taken an oath to represent his client, to protect and preserve the legal rights of his client, was sleeping to the point of snoring. I rolled my eyes in disgust as I gently touched his shoulder. He didn't move. I shook him harder! Still no response. I sighed as I balled my hand into a fist and punched his arm. He opened his eyes.

"Oh, sorry. What did I miss?" Ira Green asked me as he straightened his tie and looked around while clearing his throat.

"Do you think you can hold off with the sleeping until cross-examination?" I asked with anger.

"I apologize, Anthony."

I shook my head in disgust. What do you say to something like that?

"Mr. Green, are you ready to cross-examine?" Judge Kreindler asked.

I watched as Chris's lawyer walked back to his table. My lawyer stood up. He was still clearing his throat as he walked around the table.

"Yes, I am, Your Honor. My good citizens," Ira Green began, as he walked to the middle of the room. "I see that my esteemed colleague, Peter Brownksi, has expressed himself beautifully. Don't you think? Good afternoon, Ms. Van Buren. You say you know Anthony. A friend? Correct?"

"Well…"

"Is he your friend or not, Ms. Van Buren?" Ira Green asked.

"He's—"

"No, he's not, is he not?' Ira Green interjected.

"Your Honor, I object. Mr. Green is not giving the witness time to answer the question. He is badgering the witness!" Peter Bronski snapped.

"Sustained. Mr. Green, give the witness time to answer the question," Judge Kreindler said.

"I'm sorry. Ms. Van Buren, had you or Anthony or Chris ever been on an evening event together?"

"Evening event? What does that mean?" Carolyn asked.

"Have you been on a date with either of them? Have you been on a dinner gathering with either of them?" Ira Green asked.

"No."

"Have either one of them offered to get high with you?"

"What?" Carolyn Van Buren asked.

"I object!" ADA Bronski shouted as he jumped up out of his chair, nearly knocking it over.

"Your Honor, I am merely establishing a line of questioning that the prosecutor has done behind closed doors in prompting this witness to testify. In our discovery motion, we found that Ms. Van Buren is a drug user and was motivated by a monetary gain as motivation in coming forth to point a finger at the defendants. If the money wasn't dangling in front of her nose, would she be here today?"

"Your Honor, Mr. Green is creating a line of suspicion toward the witness and nothing more," ADA Bronski said.

"Where is this questioning going, Mr. Green?" Judge Kreindler asked.

Attorney Green turned toward the bench. "Your Honor, Ms. Van Buren is a drug user and my questioning is to establish her act of coming here today as a witness for the people to remedy justice for a man killed. Or is Ms. Van Buren here in hopes of receiving a monetary reward for her act of being a good Samaritan. The defense contends that Ms. Van Buren is in this for the TIPS reward money that was given that led to the arrest and conviction in this case. Based on Ms. Van Buren's testimony thus far, she has clearly established that she has never seen the defendants, never been around them, had absolutely no contact with the defendants. At some point, one must question exactly how she could identify these men from nearly two blocks away at 4:30 in the morning and do so by name, Your Honor."

"I will allow your line of questioning," Judge Kreindler said. "Proceed."

Finally, I could feel the tide turning in our favor, I thought, as I sat on the edge of my chair, waiting for my lawyer to go deeper in his line of questioning. I wanted to see him use his over forty years of lawyer skills to find the truth. He had a moral obligation to search out the truth.

"Thank you, sir. Ms. Van Buren, are you a crack user?" Attorney Green asked.

I watched the ADA reluctantly sit back in his chair. He entwined his fingers while nervously shaking his right leg. He knew that there was something wrong with his witness but refused to acknowledge it, or was he hiding behind her flaws by creating an illusion for her.

I watched Van Buren look around nervously. She appeared lost. She was uncomfortable as her eyes searched the faces around her. Her discomfort brought comfort to me.

If it took my lawyer to delve into her drug use, then that's what was needed to prove I was innocent.

"Answer the question, Ms. Van Buren," Judge Kreindler said.

"Yes, I use crack," Van Buren said.

"Were you smoking crack on the night you say you witnessed Anthony murder the cab driver? The truth is that you weren't going to the store at that time, were you? You were actually out that night to go buy crack to feed your addiction, were you not?" Attorney Green asked.

"I…I have a problem, yes," Van Buren said. "A problem telling the truth or a problem with drugs?" Attorney Green asked. But before she could answer, Attorney Green asked, "So you were lying when you said that you were out going to the store on March 14, 1987 right?" Green asked.

"Yes, I lied about the store, but I did see them kill that man," Van Buren said. "I'm not lying about that."

"No? So you were encouraged to come forth when you found out about the one thousand dollars that was being offered for any information leading to the capture or arrest of those responsible for the death of that poor man. Right?"

"No. Well, I didn't know about any reward money. I was just trying to help," Carolyn said. "Help," shouted Attorney Green.

"Were you now? Were your eyes seeing correctly from two blocks away, in the dark, at that hour of the morning to pick out Anthony Faison and Chris Light as the men who are being accused of this horrific act? You must have superhuman vision to see that far away!"

"I object!" ADA Bronski snapped as he leaped out of his chair.

"Sustained. Mr. Green, let's not go overboard in our questioning," Judge Kreindler said.

"I apologize, Judge. Ms. Van Buren, are you sure, absolutely positive, that you witnessed Anthony Faison and Chris Light commit this brutal crime?" Attorney Green asked.

"Yes," Carolyn Van Buren said with no hesitation.

"I have no further questions for this witness, Your Honor," Mr. Green said, as he walked back to the defense table.

Judge Kreindler rapped his hammer. "This will conclude our day, ladies and gentlemen. Tomorrow, you will have closing arguments. Thank you all for your patience. Please do not talk about the events of this case among each other," he said.

Everyone stood up as the judge exited the courtroom.

As I sat on the correctional bus that was taking me back to Rikers Island, I had a lot on my mind. How could they convict me with a crack addict as a witness? Something like that would never happen in today's society. I closed my eyes as the thought of going back to that lonely cell filled my mind. I began to pray for strength.

The weekend went quick for me. I had a visit from Sherry Saturday morning. I'd been thinking about getting heavy with her with some questions and didn't want my mother and sister there to blow my concentration. Some things in life a man likes to do with a personal touch.

I lay on my paper-thin cot and waited for the cell bars to open for my visit. Two hours later, I was sitting in the visiting room in prison jumpsuit watching Sherry approach. Damn, she was sexy. Nothing but all woman at the age of nineteen. I watched men in the visiting room stare as she casually made her way toward me. Prison had a way of making a woman look ten times better than you would remember them when you haven't had the presence of one in so long. You appreciate them more. Sherry was drop-dead fine, but looking at her now, she was even more beautiful with my lack of having sexual relations with a woman in so long.

"Hey, baby. How are they treating you?" Sherry asked, as she kissed me deliciously on my lips while sliding her tongue in my mouth. "I dropped off a hundred and fifty dollars for you in your account."

"Thank you," I said, as I watched her gingerly sit down.

She was wearing a little short, black skirt, a white blouse with two buttons open, revealing the red lace bra underneath it. Her thick thighs were glistening with lotion and made my mouth water as my heart raced rapidly with thoughts of tossing her on the table and sexually ravishing her. Yeah, I know that's a lot, but the lack of caress against a woman's skin could become suffocating at times. Yet I was a strong man in my endeavors and would hold my own as to regarding the tenderness of a woman at that moment. I had to blink out those things from my mind. I didn't have time for thinking of things I could not have. If I lost my way, I would become like so many other men in prison. Looking for nothing but always wanting everything with no hope of receiving anything.

"How was the ride over the bridge? Brothers still trying to get at you?" I asked, as she leaned forward and took my hands into her own. "I know I would be trying my best to get with you out there in the streets."

Sherry smiled. "Are you trying to question me without questioning me to see if I'm out there messing around, Mr. Faison?"

She'd always been a bright one, I thought, as I laughed while she smiled at me.

"Relax, baby. I'm committed to you and your son. That's it," she said, as she squeezed my hand for reassurance. "Your trial was intense Friday. Who would take the word of a crack addict? You're going to beat this, Shan, don't you worry about a thing."

Sure, I was sitting in front of her, displaying that bravado that every man lets kick in when we're in an unknown gray area of our lives, but deep down, I wasn't feeling my lawyer, the judge, the jury, nor the judicial system at that moment. I was looking at twenty-five years to life, and no one was going to do that time with me. No one was going to wake up each morning for twenty-five years but me. No one was going to be told what to do for the next twenty-five years but me, so if I appeared confident to my son's mother that was a sham because deep down, I was scared.

"I brought pictures of Antwan," Sherry said.

I watched her dig into her large purse and pull out the pictures. There had to be about twenty of them. She leaned over toward me and began explaining each picture to me. As she did, I took in the smell of her breathtaking perfume. My head swooned from the sweetness and its intoxicating pungency. I looked at her. I mean not just lustfully, but I took in every inch of her from head to toe. She was loyal. I knew that. My sister had told me that Sherry would mostly be at our place during the week, and she didn't think she was messing around. She was dedicated to me. I could feel it, and I respected her for the effort.

"Would you marry me, Sherry?" I asked. It came out so quickly, I had to ask myself who said it.

She stopped talking and stared at me intensely.

"I know my situation is crazy. But it could be different come Monday when I go for my verdict. I'm not saying that your answer should be based on that. I'm just saying what it is, and that is me loving you, Sherry."

Man, I could've said some other slick, street lingo to impress her, but I was being real about my feelings for this woman, who'd given me a son and was riding with me on the bogus charge I was being accused of doing. She did not stress me when there were times that she could've. Sherry was mature for her age, and she routinely showed her unconditional loyalty to me and my family. She could have told me to kiss her ass and left me doing time, but she did not and I respected and loved her for that affectionate display of kindness.

She continued to stare at me. I was getting nervous. Was it the right time to ask her to take my hand in marriage? When is the right time when you're in jail? Damn, I hope I hadn't played myself. I was starting to get uncomfortable.

"So the answer is no, huh?" I began. *Why would it be anything but that*, I thought, as I sat back in my chair dejectedly. "I can't blame you for saying no, Sherry. If the situation was reversed, would I marry you if you were facing all this time?"

"Anthony, shut up," Sherry said.

"You don't have to act like that. I—"

"I will marry you, Anthony. If you'd asked me to marry you the first day after you'd been arrested, I would've said yes," Sherry said, as she leaned toward me and wrapped her arms around my neck. "Silly. Where am I going?"

I felt a sense of warmth that I hadn't felt in a very long time. The coldness that had engulfed me for the past year of my incarceration was receding momentarily as I continued to hug the woman who was going to be my wife. I felt alive!

After the visit, I went back to the cell and did some legal research and wrote a couple of letters to the Internal Affairs complaining that I was being framed and that the arresting police had to be a part of this fabrication that was threatening to take twenty-five years of my life.

When Monday morning arrived, I was waiting for Chris to walk into the holding cell in the Brooklyn Supreme Court. I had gotten there before him. I was wearing a nice black suit with a burgundy shirt and black tie and shoes. My sister had left it for me the previous Friday while I was in court. Chris walked in wearing a brown suit. I watched as he stood by the bars, a perpetual frown shadowing his face.

"So this is it, huh?" Chris asked. He didn't look at me as if I was the one who'd gotten us in this predicament. "You think it looks good for us?"

I opened my mouth to answer him when the CO called out our names. It was time to hear the verdict from the jury.

As Chris and I walked into the courtroom, I couldn't feel anything. I mean, there are times when you can walk into a situation and have a sense of what might take place, but I felt nothing, an empty void of no possibilities. Our lawyers were waiting at the defense table. Their faces were blank as to what to expect. I walked to my table and sat down.

I leaned into my lawyer's right shoulder and whispered into his ear. "What do you think, Mr. Green?" I asked.

He turned toward me and shrugged.

I shook my head. This was my lawyer. An old fossil in modern time that should have retired twenty years ago, I thought, as I turned away in disgust.

The judge entered the chamber, and we all stood up. My hands were beginning to sweat as I watched him. He presented no threatening manner and why should he, I surmised. He was only there to administer the law and nothing more.

"Good morning, gentlemen," Judge Kreindler said as he sat down.

Everyone followed his direction by sitting down as well.

"Officer, please escort the jury in," Judge Kreindler said.

I sat at the table, nervously shaking my leg. In my heart, I knew we were going to be found not guilty. It was only right. We hadn't committed the crime we were being accused of. Faith in the judicial system was my comfort zone.

While the jury entered the courtroom, I tried to gauge their sense of where they were leaning as to the verdict. They all possessed stone faces. Poker players who wouldn't reveal their hand until called on. I couldn't get a grip on either of their faces. They all sat down without an inkling of what they'd decided.

"Good morning, jury. Have you reached a verdict?" Judge Kreindler asked.

"Yes, Your Honor," a small, bald, white man said as he stood up. He was wearing a plain white, striped shirt, and black-brown pants. "Our decision has been unanimous."

"Defendants, please rise," Judge Kreindler asked. "What is the verdict, Foreman?"

My throat became tight as I watched this man about to determine the future of my life. Either it was freedom or imprisonment. There was no other option. There were no gray areas. No in-betweens.

"Your Honor," the small, bald, white man began, "we find the defendants, Anthony Faison and Chris Light *guilty* of murder in the second degree. *Guilty* of weapons possession in the second degree and *guilty* of robbery in the third degree."

My legs went weak as I heard the verdict. My mouth went dry, and I could feel perspiration running down my back. A shiver took hold of my entire body. The bastards had found me guilty! Guilty of what? I was being railroaded!

I looked over at Chris. He was staring at the ceiling.

"Thank you, Foreman," Judge Kreindler said. "I will impose sentencing at this time. Mr. Faison and Chris Light, you have been found guilty by your peers for the crimes of murder. I will impose a sentence for Mr. Faison to the extent of twenty years to life, and for the weapons possession, you shall serve seven years, and for the robbery, you shall receive five years to run concurrent. As for Mr. Light, your sentence will be fifteen years to life and seven for the robbery. These are the sentences imposed by me in accordance with the State of New York."

I was stunned. I'd just heard my life taken from me by a man who didn't know anything about me. By a judicial system that failed to properly give me a fair and just trial. I shook my head in shock and disgust.

"I want to ask the judge a question," I said to my lawyer.

"What?" Ira Green asked. "Whatever it is, hold it until we begin the appeal process."

"No!" I hissed with anger. "I want to ask him now!"

Attorney Green looked at me with an arched eyebrow. It was obvious by his expression that he was witnessing a side of me that he'd never seen before.

"Do it," I whispered.

"Your Honor, my client would like to say a word," Mr. Green said.

Judge Kreindler looked up from the papers he was signing. "What is it, Mr. Faison?" he asked.

I took a quick glance behind me. My mother, sister, and Sherry were sitting several rows behind me. I could see that they'd taken my guilty verdict just as hard as I had as I watched the three of them crying. I turned back toward the judge.

"Your Honor, I would like to ask you to grant me permission to marry my girlfriend who is the mother of my son," I said. I made sure my voice was loud and clear. I wanted to let the judge know that although they'd found me guilty, I wouldn't let that break my spirit. "She's a wonderful woman, and I…I love her."

Judge Kreindler looked out into the benches, and then he looked at me. "Mr. Faison, you are about to enter a place that will be your home for the next twenty years if not more, depending on your living conditions and your acceptance of that environment. How would this young woman fare in such an ordeal? Why would you place her in that environment? You say you love her, but that love has to come with the realization that you are going away for a very long time, Mr. Faison. I don't want to appear callous, but I just imposed a sentence of life upon you and with such a sentence in the eyes of the court you are legally dead. Your request is *denied*."

I was crushed. All the air went out of my lungs. I felt the room around me spin for a minute. I had to grip the table with both hands to stop from screaming at the man in front of me who was wearing the black ceremonial robe for fairness. Where was the fairness in not letting me marry the woman I loved and who loved me? This was justice. To me, it was failure of justice, and I would fight it until it freed me or killed me.

I heard a wailing sound of pain. I turned to see Sherry running out of the courtroom. The sounds of her crying crushed me. I began to think frantic. I should run behind her—wait.

"Mr. Faison. Mr. Light. I hope your lives change considerably with the passing of time, and that you ask God for forgiveness," Judge Kreindler said.

Chris and I were led out of the courtroom. I glanced back at my family that was sobbing and holding each other, so did Chris. I saw his mother and sister stunned in their seats. We were both looking at spending most of our lives in prison, and there was nothing we could do to change it at the moment. A fact that was obvious as I watched my lawyer wave at me while telling me he would appeal my conviction. I knew if I depended on Ira Green for my freedom, I would spend every day of that twenty-year sentence in prison going crazy. No, I would have to find my own strength as well as my own purpose to seek my justice because the justice I'd been given was justice that was filled with darkness. There was no light within that sphere.

The Bell Tolls

(Fall and Summer 1988-1990)

I was transferred to Downstate Correctional Facility in upstate New York two weeks later. Downstate was a processing facility for state inmates. There I sat down with medical doctors who wanted to know my medical history. I spoke to psychologists who asked questions pertaining to my mother, father, sister, and brother. I had images of black blotches given to me and asked what did I see in them. I was given several pairs of pants, shirts, t-shirts, underwear, socks, sneakers, and black boots. State Prison colors was green. On the left hand side of my shirt pocket was written my last name and my state identification number. That number was my real identification. Two people could have the same first and last name, but only one would have a certain number. Cattle I'd become, and my state number was my branding iron.

One morning, I was in the cell reading some legal papers, my research into my case had become very intense. I had to prepare legal arguments for my direct appeal of my conviction. It was nonstop, and over the months, I had written hundreds of letters to various agencies and political representatives regarding protesting my conviction. The cell door opened and I stuck my head out.

"Faison! You have a visit," the CO shouted down at me from the control booth at the end of the tier.

It was a Tuesday. Who would be visiting me? I asked myself as I went and brushed my teeth. I hadn't grown used to wearing the state green prison uniforms. I thought that they were clothing of guilt. And feeling that way, I urged my family to send me clothing that I felt comfortable wearing. Sure, I had to wear the green pants, but everything else would be street clothing and not prison issued.

It was my psychological acceptance of my situation as well as my rejection toward my false imprisonment. Ten minutes later, a CO came and escorted me to the visiting room. Our walk to the visiting room was a short one. I watched two large doors opened in front of me. I could see that the room was very large as I entered it. I looked around the room. I saw a man raise his arm and wave at me. It was my father.

I walked over. My father stood up and shook my hand. It was good to see my old man, I thought, as I stood there staring at him. Most people say we look alike. I, as the son, couldn't see it. We hugged for a moment, and then we sat down across from each other.

"I'm surprised to see you here, Pop," I said.

"You know me, boy. I like to keep things to the simplest equations, and this isn't my comfort zone," he said.

I watched him look around the visiting room. He was thinking. Whenever he grew quiet, I knew that he was trying to think of his next question. My father could be a complicated man. I had watched him as a little boy while idolizing everything about him. He was the only real man I knew as a child. He would tell me and my brother that black men were near extinction because of the hate men not of color had for men of color. I never understood what he was talking about until I became older and saw what life was like as a young black male growing up in an urban environment. My father had once told me he'd been a part of the Black Panther Movement during his younger days before he went off to war. He did not preach to me or my brother; he would enlighten us with little antecedents. My father was never a talkative man. If he didn't have anything constructive to say, then he didn't say anything. I'd never seen my father display anger toward any man as a child. He said that all men should be respected regardless of their race, faith, or nationality. His philosophy was simple: you die the way you live.

"This prison life is not you, Anthony. I thought I raised you better than this. I taught you and your brother to be respectful, courteous, and to think like chess experts in this sick game of life. Now I'm looking across at you wearing prison greens. As a little boy, I used to love watching you take apart things with your hands and then put them back together again without any instructions. You've always been bright, son. What is this all about?"

I rubbed my hands across my face. When I brought them down, my father was staring at me. The pain in his face was obvious. It was a look of a father who'd lost faith in his son.

"Dad, this is crazy. I—"

"Anthony, with patience, a man like me can wait, but do not take my patience for granted, you're still not old enough for me to knock you to the floor. So your answer better be truthful. Did you kill that man?"

With the most sincere expression I could muster, I stared at the man I loved and gave him my deepest and fulfilling answer. "Dad, I swear—"

"No need to use God's allegiance at this time, Anthony. Just tell me what's in your heart, son."

I began shaking my head. I looked him straight in the eyes. "Dad, I did not kill that man. I didn't do any of the things they say I did."

My father stared at me. His eyes never blinked as he held my eyes for what seemed like forever. As I stared at my father, I noticed how there were more gray hairs in his beard and sprinkled throughout his hair. What was he now? Fifty? Forty-eight, I guessed. He was aging. We, as children, forget that as we age, our parents age even faster. My father was a good man. I loved and respected him very much and would never want to lose his respect and faith in me.

"Okay, son, I believe you. I wanted to hear it from you and look into your eyes when you said it. You know your mother and I have our ups and downs, but we'll be looking to get you a private lawyer soon to get this craziness over with as quickly as we can."

"Pop, lawyers have a tendency to drain the pockets of loved ones, only to have the case thrown back to them. I have really been studying criminal law, and I could be my own lawyer as far as filing the proper legal motions is concerned. Let me see what I can do from behind these bars first before you start throwing money to the three-piece suit wolves that are sitting around waiting for prey like you."

My father laughed. It was always a good thing to see, his laugh. His laugh could make any person sitting beside him laugh. "I like how you think, son," he said.

"At this stage, Dad, I can only think one way," I said.

He nodded. "Listen to me. These correction officers up in these woods don't give a damn about a man of color, Latino, black, or Indian. To them, they're all niggers. Most of these rednecks further up in these unknown counties will kill a man of color rather than feed them if they get out of hand. I want you to take care of yourself every waking day, and don't be too quick to give someone your trust. You trust a person in here, you better make damn sure it's someone that will be there for you when it gets hot and sticky. You hear me, son."

"Sure, Dad. I will make sure I'm always on my toes," I said.

"Okay, let's talk about the family. I saw that fat grandson of mine a few days ago. He's starting to lose the family resemblance and look more like his mother, son."

"How's Monique? Did you see her, Pop?"

"I saw her. She's going to grow up to be a fine young lady. She's quiet, but respectful. I will look after them, son."

From that moment on, I sat back and enjoyed the company of my father as he talked about his children growing up and how he was growing up in some ways as well. We talked frankly to each other, not like father and son, but man to man. It was the best conversation I'd ever had with my father in a very long time, and it felt invigorating.

As our time together came to a close, I really took in the image of the man I would probably grow to be one day. My father possessed a strong chin and a will of iron. If he was wrong about something, he admitted it, but if he was right, then not even the strongest person in the world could get him to back down.

"Son, I think they're kicking your old man out."

My father, with his cynical wit, began to rise from his seat. I also stood up as the COs announced that the visiting hours were over in ten minutes. Now that I really looked at my father, I saw that I'd grown a foot taller than I'd remember him.

"Sometimes, we sacrifice what we don't want to do for what is right. I left you some money before coming in here. You make sure the bastards don't steal it."

"I'll count my change like you taught me, Pop," I said.

He nodded as he stared at me.

As if on cue, we both reached over and hugged one another.

"I love you, son," my father whispered in my ear as he pulled away.

"I love you too, Pop," I said as my father smiled and turned away.

I watched him walk away with his back straight. An old man with yesterday's thoughts and concepts, I admitted. Prideful and strong was his way of thinking. A good man with a good heart.

Gladiator School is the title of a prison I went to after six weeks in Downstate. It had incurred that name from the many young men who'd first encountered it in the late seventies and early eighties. Its official name was Great Meadows Correctional in Comstock, New York. It was located in a small town upstate. Rumor had it that the name Gladiator School came from the many race wars and gang fights that resulted in loss of life for many disillusioned inmates caught up in a lifestyle doomed from the beginning. There were so many stabbing from weapons buried in the dirt that prison officials blacktarred the entire yard to prevent further deaths.

By the end of 1989, I had settled in to a ritual that had begun at the beginning of that year. It was fall, and I'd sworn to myself that no day would pass that I would not protest my innocence. I knew that using the collect calls phone program would not work. I would write every night as many letters as I could to anyone I thought would listen, anyone I thought could help me. I would regularly go to the law library and get the names of politicians like congressman, senators, ex-judges, clergymen and women, community activists, and any other person I thought who could see my plight. I would start each letter with a simple introduction:

Dear Sir/Madam,

I know you have probably heard the story of men saying they were innocent of the charges against them, but I write to you herein, wrongfully imprisoned for a crime that I did not commit.

This was the beginning of all my letters as I added other facts to my case in the letters. If I didn't write at least twenty letters a night, I couldn't sleep. Writing had become my passion. When other inmates turned their lights out for the night to sleep, my lights came on and stayed on till I saw the sun rise through the prison bars. I wrote letters all night and done so by hand. Each night I began in prayer, and each morning ended in prayer. I knew that God heard my cries if not no one else.

One Saturday morning, I awoke to the sounds of a new neighbor in the next cell beside me. The night previously I'd heard the cell bars open, but I was too focused on my writing to care. Besides, it was a survival tactic not to be nosy in prison. If you were too nosy, you could find an inch of your nose missing from the prospect of someone cutting it off. A person never asked another man why he was doing time. That question could get a man's heart punctured with a shank or a few stitches down the side of their face from a razor for inquiring about something that was none of their business. I had come to understand the laws within prison, and I respected them to survive. Prison life was a hard life that could either eat you up or break you down to the lowest denominator in the equation of life. Its shell of emptiness and it makes a person empty if they hold on to things outside of the prison wall. It's a cold place with a combination of cold men who would rather stab you than befriend you. I would come to see these things and walk among them with caution.

The cell bars opened. It was breakfast time, and everyone that was going to breakfast stepped out onto the tier. The person who'd moved in last night's cell bars did not open. He wasn't going to breakfast. I stepped in front of his cell. I wanted to make sure I was not being celled next to a man who might have mental issues, and one day might decide he wants to start stabbing people. I didn't want to step into a shank as I exited my cell any day in the future.

"What's up?" I said as I stood in front of my neighbor's cell bars. I made sure not to get too close in case the man had an issue with space. "You came in last night, huh? My name is Shan." In prison, inmates did not like other inmates calling them by the government name, i.e., birth name. Nicknames were like real names, everyone had one.

My new neighbor looked me up and down. Sizing me up. I guess he wanted to know who was I to be standing in front of his cell bars, introducing myself. He stared at me for a minute without saying a word. I thought he might've been a mute.

"Yeah, ahright. My name is Critter."

"You're not coming out for breakfast?" I asked. Trying to see what I was working with. "They have the powdered eggs, biscuits, milk, and their special turkey ham."

"No," Critter said.

His words were brisk. "Where you coming from?" I asked.

"Auburn," Critter said as he turned away and walked to the back of his cell.

"I've been told Auburn was a laid-back prison. Why did you leave there?" I asked.

"Fighting."

"Oh, so you coming out of SHU," I inquired.

Critter nodded.

"Well, not trying to tell you how to do your bid, but Comstock doesn't play that. If you get too out of hand, the doctors will shoot you up with some medication and throw you in the psych ward. Unfortunately for inmates, the court has repeatedly affirmed this inhumane act. I found out that this is a disciplinary prison. So if I was you, I'd take it slow," I said.

Critter nodded again.

"Ahright," I said. "They're forming the line downstairs for breakfast. I'll see you later."

Critter didn't say a word. He nodded and watched me walk away.

He was a strange one, I thought, as I got in line at the bottom tier, which was called the flats. I was locked in Cell Block area B. Everyone had to form a line at the bottom of the flats. The COs in Comstock controlled everything. If inmates went into the mess hall, they went through metal detectors. If inmates went to a visit, they went through metal detectors. Comstock controlled all movement of inmates in the prison. Old timers still in the prison would talk how Comstock had once been controlled by the inmates in the early eighties. There were stories of inmates fighting every day in the prison until guards simply let them get it out their systems, and when they were finished, the one standing would be the one charged with assault and the one lying in the dirt would be the victim. He would get his ass beat again, but this time from the guards. Yet those times had come to an end with the new oversight board enacted by the Commissioner of Corrections due to the many assaults and deaths and violence. This all eventually led to more metal detectors and random body searches every day.

Returning to my cell after breakfast thirty minutes later, I glanced in on Critter. I don't know, I thought the brother was cool. Although I just met him, he was quiet with a strong aura about him that I liked. He appeared to be a standup brother. I hardly felt that way about people who I came in to contact with. Too many deceptive people in prison who live to exploit you for the smallest things, which eventually would lead to a bloody confrontation. I called my thinking the mover's effect. I never let myself become involved with prison politics. I stayed to myself and carried myself like the man I was.

As I watched the cell bars close behind me, I stood there for a moment contemplating what to say to Critter. I didn't want him to think I was a pest or anything like that. "Yo, Critter, you know next week, they'll be calling you to place you in a program," I said.

I heard Critter coming to the bars. "If they ask you, tell them you want to go to the welding shop."

"Why welding? I've never welded before," Critter said.

"Man, none of us has any skills in welding. We're all from the ghetto, but it's more like a handout class that everyone goes to for the latest hearsay of what's going on in the prison," I said.

"Okay, I'll tell them," Critter said.

I think that day sealed my friendship with Critter. He had a demeanor about him that was quick to see and appreciate. I couldn't put my finger on it right then and there, but there was trust in him that I immediately picked up on. I can't explain it, but it was there.

Three months later, Critter and I had become joined at the hip. I found someone who did not play the friendship games, try to manipulate me. With Critter, I had a sounding board that gave me advice and showed me a different outlook as to my surrounding and my situation. I could tell that he did not just come to prison and that this was not his first time.

"Man, look around us. Prison is a warehouse of flesh, and the key holders are second generation deviates," Critter said.

I laughed; we were walking the yard. Prison had become nothing more than holding pens for angry black and Latino men who were waiting to get out and destroy everything they felt had betrayed them.

"Is that Mathematics?" Critter asked.

I looked to the right of me where Critter had pointed. He was right. It was Mathematics. I shook my head as I watched Mathematics argue with another Five Percenter. Mathematics weighed one hundred and twenty pounds soaking wet, but his mouth ran like he was over six feet, five inches, and two hundred and sixty pounds. I usually didn't get involved with disputes, but Mathematics was like a kid in a smaller kid's body. He was twenty-two years old and spoiled. His parents gave him anything he wanted. Yet here he was doing time like any other hoodlum. Story was that he wanted to be a street kid instead of a good kid and ran with some heavy-duty young boys in Brooklyn doing armed robberies. Their lifestyle was opposite of his. He liked that style and was now doing a three-to-six bid.

"Let's walk over there and calm Math down," I said.

"For what? Mathematics has a big mouth for someone so little, Shan. He won't be satisfied until someone put some metal in his little ass," Critter commented.

I smiled. Critter was right. There had been many disputes that I had to settle for Mathematics over the past three months I had to keep others from hurting him. "I know, but walk with me anyway," I said.

Together, Critter and I walked over to the circle in which there were several other God Bodies (Five Percenters) surrounding Mathematics. I could see that Mathematics was having a heated debate with another God Body by the name of Infinite. By the gist of the story, they were arguing about the creation of the world. Convicted felons standing around in a prison yard debating, and of all things, the creation of the world. Mathematics was animated to the point that he was flailing his arms around to make his point. He could be dramatic like that. Always wanted the last word.

Let me explain to you what a God Body is. The numeric number one hundred can be broken down into a simple equation of three parts in which a man with supreme knowledge would be able to decipher. There is the eighty-five percent of the world who could be considered not knowledgeable to the way of the world. They wore a veil of ignorance. They would be considered the blind sheep. Then there is the ten percent of men who possess extreme knowledge but refuse to enlighten those of less knowledge because they deemed them to be unfit to digest the magnitude of what the world has to offer. And of course, there remains the five percent who make it their moral obligation to bring peace and enlightenment into the lives of men and woman living in darkness by exposing the evil by men who are not of color. All God Body were given lessons to learn. Each lesson learned was an elevation of knowledge.

"Math, what's up?" I asked. I looked around at the faces in the circle. There were a few God Bodies I knew. Those that knew me acknowledge me with a nod of their head. "Why are you making a scene, man?"

"No, Shan, we're just building, man," Mathematics said, as he stepped out of the circle.

"Yeah, man, but look at how the COs are looking over here. Let's go," I said. For some reason, I'd immediately taken Mathematics under my wing. Although he was a couple of years younger than me, he had a mentality of a fourteen year old. And since he was from Marcy Projects, where I spent a considerate amount of my youth there at my cousin's house, I felt I had to at least try to keep him in line. "You need to calm down sometimes before your antics get you in trouble, bro."

Mathematics said peace to the circle of men and walked away with us as we began to walk around the yard. It was spring. The warmth in the air had everyone feeling antsy. Whenever the summer time kicked in, men locked up become caged lunatics. Anything and everything could spark a fight, a stabbing, or a riot in a blink of an eye. The tension in prison could be as thick as trying to cut through a rubber mat with a plastic knife.

"Hey, there goes the Preppy Killer heading out to another visit," Critter said, as he pointed to the young white man being escorted out of the yard by two COs. If killing a white girl can get you that much attention, as a society of humans, we are lost.

Critter and Mathematics laughed at his sleight humor. I looked on as the person they were talking about, Robert Chambers, smiled and waved whenever some inmate called out his name. I couldn't understand how a killer like him received more attention in a positive way for a crime that made national news and still had a female following from all over the world fighting to visit him. It's ironic and sad, I thought, as I continued walking the yard.

As we walked the yard, we talked about everything that came to mind. Prison did that to a person. You think about the what ifs, the maybes, and anything else that would temporarily take your mind out of the cesspool of madness. I watched as Bostic hurried over toward us. Bostic was cool. He was a young man who made a person laugh. His story of imprisonment was the oddest one I'd ever heard. He'd been found guilty of murder when he was fourteen years old. Being of such a young age, the judicial system had to watch him grow into adulthood by placing him in juvenile facilities before sending him to a maximum security prison like Comstock to serve his twenty-five to life sentence. I'd read about Bostic's legal case. It was because of him and his case that the courts changed the law to indict and prosecute minors as adults at the very young age of sixteen. Bostic, although unaware at the time, had made history with his act of butchery.

"What's up?" Bostic said as he approached. "Mathematics, why is it your little ass always getting into beefs, man? Shut your mouth sometimes, man. You talk too much!"

"Fuck you, Bostic!" Mathematics snapped as he stormed off apparently offended by Bos's comment.

"Come on, Bostic, you know he's young," I said. "If we continue going at him like that, he's just going to keep doing what he's doing without understanding why he does what he does."

"Yeah, you're right. I'm going to apologize to the punk," Bostic said as he broke into a small trot after Mathematics.

Critter and I watched Bostic run after Mathematics for a moment, and then we started walking again.

"Critter, I have to tell you something," I began. Critter glanced at me. "Man, I didn't do this crime. I'm doing twenty years to life for something I didn't do. It's tearing me apart inside with every day that I'm in here."

Critter stopped. He turned toward me, and in his eyes, I could see the compassion. "Look, Shan. Everyone in prison is saying they didn't commit a crime. No matter how many times you tell a person that story, it means nothing. If you want people to believe you, then you have to prove it and not keep saying it over and over again. Me, I don't care if you did it or not, we still cool. As for wanting people to take notice of your situation, you have to shout it out, and then people will see you. Your shouts must be heard behind these prison walls. Anything short of that is meaningless," he said.

He didn't wait for me to respond; he simply began walking away. I stood there for a moment, gathering my thoughts, and then caught up to him. I did not speak though. He was right. I had to take the world by the back of its head and force my freedom down its throat.

Critter could be wise beyond his twenty-five years, but then he could be the funniest man in prison. For the past five months, he'd been telling me that he was getting out of Comstock. That he'd devised a plan to get a transfer. I told him that wouldn't be possible. I'd been there for nearly two years by now, and everyone that came there had to do a year before requesting a transfer. By this time, he'd only been there for nine months.

One evening after dinner, Critter called me to come to the cell bars. I was in the cell composing a letter to send to the Congressman Floyd Flake. I had written him several times in the past, but he only responded once. I wanted him to write the Brooklyn District Attorney Charles J. Hynes and request that further investigation be conducted into my claims of misconduct by the arresting officers. I went to the bars, and Critter began to whisper to me that tonight, he was going to make his move for a transfer.

Standing there, I was startled when I heard Critter began screaming.

"CO?" Critter began. "I need to see a doctor!"

"Critter, you know what you're doing?" I whispered. My concern was obvious as I listened to him continue to scream.

"Yeah," he said as other inmates began to scream for the CO as well. "It was a rule that every inmate followed: if the screams for a CO pierced the night from a cell, all inmates kept screaming until a CO came. A loud clunk sounded as a gate opened, and all the lights came on. A CO yelled out from the bottom tier, "Yeah, what do you want?" I yelled out Critter's cell number and began hearing the COs begin to run. When they arrived in front of his cell and said, "What's the problem, inmate?" Critter said, "I keep having these dreams with blood all over my body, and white people dead at my feet!"

I ran to the back of the cell and exploded with laughter. *Critter done lost his damn mind,* I said to myself. "Critter, you're not going to get a transfer with that. They're gonna put your ass in the psych ward for sure," I said to myself, between breaths. My side was hurting from laughter so hard that I fell back onto the bed.

Critter continues yelling, "Get me out of here, CO. Blood is coming out of the walls," and as other COs arrived, Critter's cell door opened and he was asked to step out backward, handcuffed, and taken away. One of the men who arrived had on a white medical jacket, and he began to ask Critter questions. "Do you feel like killing yourself?" Then he asked, "Would you like to take a walk with me?" and Critter replied that he would. Critter was escorted off the tier with four COs and a doctor.

When they reached the end of the tier to leave, I screamed out in laughter as did several other inmates who overheard what was going on. I said this to myself, "This motherfucker done lost his mind for real," then laughed some more.

Forty-eight hours later, I was still laughing from time to time as the images of Critter popped into my mind. Four days had passed and I began to worry now. Did he play that crazy game too damn good, and they'd doped him up with some medication? Or did they beat him down for trying to act up and threw him in a cell somewhere? I tried to get information out of the COs on my tier, but they said they didn't know Critter's whereabouts. This was getting serious, I thought. They knew where he was, they were just being deceptive because I was asking about him.

Several days later, I didn't know what to think. I would be writing my letters as I did every day and hear cell doors open on the tier. I would grab my paper-thin plastic mirror and stick it out the bars to get a view of the tier and who was on it. It wasn't Critter. The next morning—like I'd been doing for the past several days, I would look on the new arrival sheet that was posted near the CO's booth. It disclosed all movement in the prison that day in or out of the prison. On this particular morning, I was relieved. I saw Critter's government name. He was being brought back to the cell block, but placed on the flats.

By the time lunch time arrived, Critter was in his cell. Being that he was on the flats and all the tiers had to line up on the flats, I would see him. I sent Freedom, a brother who I knew from my neighborhood, to take Critter some cans of food and tell him to come to the yard later on that afternoon.

When late afternoon rolled around and everyone began filling the yard, I'd been outside already pacing the yard. I was hoping Critter wouldn't come outside looking like a deranged, drugged-out zombie from taking medication. I knew Comstock's policy. If they couldn't handle an inmate, they found a doctor to administer enough medication in that person to keep the man docile. They did not care if it was legal or not.

I clearly remember this practice being used on Howard Pappy Mason; he was a drug dealer originally from Crown Heights Brooklyn near the Albany Projects, hustled in Queens with Fat Cat. Was accused of ordering a hit on his parole officer and then on a New York City police officer protecting a witness in a drug case. He was housed in F-Block, which was known to be the worse Special Housing Unit (SHU) in the entire State of New York. Twenty-three hour lock in, no windows, no contact with other inmates or your family, no personal property in you cell, and it was Pappi Mason who was the first to be drugged based upon the fear that correction officials had of him. Not just him, but the influence that he had over the prison population. Pappy was an icon in prison. Strangely enough, cop killers are revered in prison. However, after Pappy had a sergeant attacked in general population while he was in F-Block, prison officials sent the doctors in on him. It was not long before word got out that Pappy had stop eating, stop bathing, and was eating his own feces. No longer a threat. The message was clear.

My wait wasn't long. I saw the side profile of someone who resembled Critter come out surrounded by others. As I strained my eyes to make sure it was him, I smiled when I saw the ears of the person I thought was him. Critter had ears like Yoda in *Star Wars*. I watched him looking around as he walked farther into the yard.

"Critter," I called out to him. He turned at the sound of his name.

I watched as he had his Harlem stride toward me. He looked okay as he neared me, but I had to hear how he talked to be sure he was okay.

"What's up, man?" I asked as he walked up on me. "Man, what the fuck! "Where in the hell have you been, bro?"

"Whew, man, the bastards had me on the other side of the prison in an open cell. Damn COs sat in front of my cell when I pissed, dropped a load, farted, masturbated, or whatever. I couldn't even put a sheet over the bars for at least a little privacy. What kind of crap was that?"

I simply stared at him as he described his experience.

"So the psych doctor came to my cell after about three days. I'm looking at this white man wearing a pair of thick glasses as he asks me do I need any medication or if I'm going to kill myself. I kicked the bars and told him to get me out of the cell. The bastard jumped back and whispered something to the CO. I had to catch myself from that moment on so things wouldn't get ugly. I had to calm down, you know. I told the doctor that I had a mental bump, but I was okay. He walked back to the cell and looked into my face for a full minute, and then he told the CO to send me back to my cell. That was a close one."

I listened to Critter without blinking an eye. He spoke so fast it appeared to come out all at once. I couldn't help but laugh.

"What's up? How's prison life been without me?" Critter asked humorously.

I shook my head as I continued to laugh. I was laughing so hard I had tears rolling down my face. I shook my head as I continued to laugh. The man was crazy, but he had a good heart.

"Yo! You got food in your cell?" Critter asked. "The fools wouldn't let me go to commissary."

"Man, didn't I tell your crazy ass that they were not going to transfer you because you wanted to act like you were losing your mind," I said. "You're lucky they didn't dope your behind up. Yeah, I have some food. I will bring you out something tonight when we have yard. Come on, let's walk. I want to talk to you."

I started walking. I heard Critter following me. Seconds later, he was walking beside me.

"What's wrong, Shan?" Critter asked. "You're having a problem with someone? Something happened, bro?"

I kept walking.

"Yo, man. What's up?" Critter continued.

I could hear the concern in his voice. I stopped and turned around to face him.

"Sherry came to see me three days ago," I began as I looked at Critter. I noticed he'd grown a full beard since being locked away. "She brought my son."

"Okay, that's good. You had a good time on the visit? Did she wear one of those short dresses you say she likes to wear when coming to see you?" Critter asked as he smiled.

I rubbed the back of my neck. My neck had been feeling tight lately. I went to the doctor earlier that week, but he told me it was probably stress, and if I relaxed more, it'd go away. How do you relax in prison? I stared at the doctor as if he done lost his mind. He must have felt my eyes burning through the back of his head, so he gave me two aspirins and told me to take two days off from my daily program. As I began to walk out of his office, the doctor said, "Faison, you can start reducing your stress by stopping worrying about things that you cannot change or influence. Most inmates suffer stress-related illnesses because they worry too much about the outside world. Simply stop." His words cut me like a knife, and I carried that scar throughout my imprisonment.

"Why are you acting strange, man? Did you or didn't you have a good time?" Critter asked.

"I had to let Sherry go." "Let Sherry go?" Critter replied with a face of confusion and concern. "She wanted to tell me herself instead of letting rumors reach me from the outside. She said that my mother and sister can bring my son up to see me and that she had to move on with her life. That she had met someone six months ago and things have gotten serious." My voice cracked a little as I told the story, and I think Critter had felt my pain. I watched his expression change from concern to anger. "It happened out of nowhere," I said.

I walked with my head down. I was distraught that my life had become more confusing with Sherry deciding to see someone else. Was I upset? Really upset? I was doing twenty years. I couldn't marry her because of my sentence and the arrogance of the judge who'd denied me from marrying her. My situation had just become even more complicated.

"Shan, I don't tell people in here my business, man, but I can understand you're suffering right now and we're cool like that. When I first started my bid in eighty-six, I met this woman. You know, she never knew me in the street, but we clicked once we did get to know each other. Her sister was dealing with one of the brothers on my tier. He introduced us. Anyway, that girl rode with me all the way to Clinton Dannemora Prison, and during that time, a year and a half, I asked her to marry me. She was happy. I mean really happy that I asked her. When I accepted my plea deal in court of seven and a half to fifteen years, I only had me to worry about to do the time. But when I asked her to marry me, I now had to take her life into consideration as well. I realized that I couldn't let her do that time with me. I had nothing to give her but emotional and psychological support from the inside. But between you and me, I think I didn't want to marry her because I didn't want the reality of her one day telling me she wanted a divorce or she couldn't do the bid with me anymore. Either way, I had to set her free so I could free myself from the burden of thinking if she was messing around with someone out there. Was she being faithful to me? So many things of negativity ran through my head at the time that I was losing her before I even had her. Bro, I couldn't do time like that. I have to do this time by myself to survive this nightmare."

"So you're telling me that—"

"Bro, I'm telling you that this pain will pass. I'm telling you that you can marry ten women, and you'd still be doing time if you're still behind these bars. I'm telling you that your total concentration should be in you giving that time back on an appeal or exonerating yourself altogether. Don't feel any pity for yourself. Don't feel any pity for Sherry. Do what you've been doing since walking into this beastly animal called prison. Prison was created for one purpose: to punish the guilt for violating society's rules. You can rehabilitate some of these men in here. Some refuse to be anything other than what they think of themselves as being. Man, make the world hear you through your writing, and to do that, you have to be able to open your mouth, your eyes, your mind, and be focused unlike anyone before you."

I nodded. Critter was right. I couldn't change the way others perceived me, but I could change the way I was being perceived by the world, and to do that, I had to press my case of being wrongfully convicted to a combustible state of mind.

I was in the law library the next day going over some material when Salvatore Bashetti walked in. He was a large man whose stomach appeared to be getting bigger every time I saw him.

"Anthony, how ya doing!" Salvatore asked.

I was behind the desk. Salvatore was followed with the baggage of two other Italians who, rumor had it, would kill for him if he told them to. With each day in prison, I realized that no matter what you do in life, your lifestyle follows you.

"Hey, Sal," I said.

Sal walked up to the counter. "I need you to handle some legal stuff for me," he said as he looked around suspiciously to make sure no one was listening. "I have a problem with a friend of mine who might be thinking of cutting a deal against me. I do not want this to go through my lawyer, can't say I really trust that bastard anyway."

I stared at Salvatore. What was he asking me? With Sal, everything was cryptic. He was either saying one thing and hoping you knew what he was saying or he was saying something altogether different, and if you didn't know what he was saying,

he continued until you grasped it. He was a capo in one of the
New York City crime families, and he displayed it with aplomb.

"My associate is trying to go in a roundabout way of nodding
his head in my direction in regard to an unknown incident he and
I had once participated in a few eons ago," Salvatore continued.
"Now if his lies were to become knowledgeable to the prosecutor,
then I might be in a finger-pointing situation that could lead to
my credibility being shadowed to parties outside these walls, if
you know what I mean?"

I continued staring at Salvatore. I didn't know what he meant.
I don't think Salvatore knew what he meant at times when talking,
but who was I to tell him different?

Salvatore sighed with impatience. "What I'm saying,
Anthony, is I need you to file some motions to ask the courts
to let me know if and when someone is implicating my name in
something and will it be used against me in the future. You know
what I mean?"

I rolled my eyes. "Sal, I didn't know what you were saying in
the beginning, but now I do. Why couldn't you say that the first
time, man?" I asked. "Get me your paperwork and I will work
on it."

Sal leaned in toward me. His voice was low. "Books have ears,
Anthony. Always remember that," he whispered.

Sal knew what most inmates did not, and that was if you
worked in the law library as a certified paralegal and you provide
legal representation or research, you are held to the very same
laws that govern attorney-client privileges. I cannot be ordered
by a court to disclose anything that Sal discussed with me, and if
a statement by a prison-certified law clerk was to enter a court, it
would be inadmissible in a court of law. Besides, my reputation
was sound.

I watched as Sal walked out of the library. One bodyguard
took the lead and the other followed. I had to laugh. Sal was

a well-respected man in Comstock. Respect is everything in prison—everything. He was feared and comical at the same time.

Salvatore was a made man that you better not take for granted and the inmates knew that if you violated him in any way, retribution will most certainly occur and that extended to your family on the outside.

A week later, I had a small reprieve as to my prison experience. I was transferred to honor block. Considering Comstock was deemed a maximum security disciplinary prison, to apply for honor block and get it was a good thing. You only had to wait three months, and if a person stayed away from the disciplinary write-ups within that time, a person could be granted access to the pleasure of cooking on a hot plate rather than using a stinger to boil water in plastic buckets. A person could also take a shower with no time limits, which, if not in honor block, consisted of five minutes on the regular tiers. Taking into consideration the easy entry into honor block was due to the prison restraints. A place like Comstock could be a thorny prison of repression with the constant searches as well as strip searches at any random time added to the arrogance of the COs toward the inmates by their actions of confronting inmates with physical harm, and when an inmate challenged their authority, he was beaten severely. This was how they maintained their dominance in a prison so far from urban neighborhoods that they could kill an inmate and bury him in a wooded grave and his family members would be told a lie as to the circumstances of his death. Honor block took away some of the tension. Not all, but enough to keep all parties amiable.

Strength of Character

(1988–1990 continued)

I began to notice things while being housed in honor block. Prison's a subliminal whore that could seduce you into thinking that it was good for you by manipulating your psyche. If you were a weak-minded person, then you thought it was fine for you to be given recognition of your exposed and confined life. It gave you the false impression that if you followed the rules and stayed out of disciplinary trouble, then you were rewarded with limited perks. I understood their manipulation. Prison forced you into understanding that it was an off-branch of society. If a person followed the laws of the land and kept a clean nose, then they would be rewarded with the better things society had to offer. It didn't take me long to grasp this reality.

I met men in honor block who had become so misled into thinking that honor block was a glorious position to be in that they forgot that they were doing time. I entered honor block because it gave me more freedom to write my letters as well as removed some restraints toward my lighting situation at night. When I was in my old block, the lights on the tier went off at eleven o'clock. I would be on my third letter by that time and had many more to go before I could climb into my small bed. My eyes would strain significantly as I tried to write in semidarkness. The little light that came from the CO's area would have me writing on the floor in the cell near the front of the bars just to make sure my words were spelled correctly. I would be on that hard concrete floor for hours every night writing my letters. There were many mornings when I awoke with raw elbows from bracing myself while sucking in as much light as I could to finish my letters. Although in pain, I refused to leave that cold, concrete floor until I had completed my letter-writing ritual.

Living in honor block, I saw men in their most vulnerable positions. There were nights while I sat in the television area watching everyone. I had to get an insight as to a judicial system that seemed to house men like cattle in a barn. But first, I wanted to know why prisons were built in places so far upstate. I once asked a CO what he would be doing if there wasn't a prison in his town. His answer shocked me. He said that prisons gave men like him hope for a better life. If there were no prisons, then he would probably be living on welfare. He was a young CO who'd been working there for five years. No older than twenty-five years old was my estimate of his age. He talked about how politicians are encouraged by their constituents in upstate counties to get prison contracts to help employ towns. I was appalled when he told me this. Yet right there at that moment, as I looked around, I could see why prisons were built so far from New York City. His statement made sense in a very honest way.

Prison brought me in to contact with men I probably wouldn't say a word to in the streets. But once getting to know them, it didn't matter what crimes they committed, because after a while, I found myself respecting the individual and not the act for which he'd been convicted of. Wait. Let me correct that. As on the streets, there is also a code of ethics in prison. Rapists and child molesters are considered the lowest thing on the human chain in prison. You can rob a man and get time. You can kill a person and get time, but if you rape or molest a child or female and it gets to the population, then you are no longer doing time; it is doing you because everyone you might come into contact with will despise you for your inhumane act against the very fabric of life. Children in prison are cherished and revered. A child can't protect itself against predators, but once imprisoned, those predators become others' prey and are condemned to years of abuse from inmates. Some even commit suicide to get away from their tormentors.

I once watched a man admit he'd raped a woman and that's why he was in prison. He appeared to be proud of his crimes. It was my first week in Comstock. I had found out through other inmates that he was the Far Rockaway Serial Rapist and had been convicted of several attacks on women. The next week, that same man was going to the mess hall to get dinner, and while on line near the counter, someone threw a pot of boiling hot grease in his face. I was ten feet away as I watched the man's skin begin to slowly peel from his face. It was horrible to watch, yet it also gave me an incentive to always be on my toes. The prison investigated the incident for two months and never found out who'd committed the brutal act. In truth, prison officials care for these type of convicts even less. As for the proud rapist, they say the hot grease had blinded him and scarred him for the rest of his life. Justice can be found in many painful forms sometimes in prison.

I'd persuaded Critter to apply for honor block. I watched one evening as he entered the room, looking around suspiciously. He'd refused for three months to apply. He kept telling me he wasn't going to do any light time. I explained to him that to me, time is time no matter how you do it or where, it all counts. He went for that especially when I told him that he could watch television inside a room that had cushion benches and not outside in the cold. I waved him over to where I was sitting.

"I filed a motion yesterday," I said as Critter sat down in a row of seats in front of me. "It was a FOIL request." "You wrote to the Fruit of Islam? Man, those brothers are not going to help you. They can't even help the men they have inside here, much less you."

I smiled as I shook my head. Maybe they should've given Critter some medication when he was in the psych ward. He could be bitterly cynical, I thought. The man's mind wandered sometimes. "No," I began patiently. "FOIL is the acronym for 'freedom of information law' request, which is simply a legal request that you submit to a state or government agency, requesting the disclosure of documents in the custody of that given agency. These documents are deemed to be public records and therefore privy under the law.

"I will be submitting these requests before the 77th Precinct in Brooklyn and the Kings County District Attorney office. I want to know if any latent fingerprints were ever found in the cab. I noticed from my research that the ADA at my trial never mentioned anything about prints. I just got this feeling," I said.

"If the precinct denies you that information, maybe they're hiding something. Why wasn't this requested during your trial?" Critter asked.

"It was actually when my lawyer filed the pre-trial disclosure motion that the ADA should have released any information or evidence that is exculpatory in nature. I didn't have a good lawyer, and the judge was prejudicial. When my lawyer requested something, the judge denied it. My trial was crazy, man."

"Okay. What's your next option?" Critter said. "My options do not change," I admitted. "I am in the fight of my life, and the journey that I must embark on is not planned, my friend. I must find my way through this and I will. I can't let anything deter me from seeking my freedom. If I were denied my request, then I would seek that information with the assistance of something or someone down the road. But giving up was not on my plate and it never would be. I would die expunging my last breathe before

I gave in to a judicial system that maliciously railroaded me. My faith had to lie within me. I could never give up believing in myself. If I did, then I would die in prison."

I called home about three weeks later to speak to my sister concerning my son and daughter. At the beginning of my sister's conversation, from the first word that came out of her mouth, I knew something was wrong. I had to stop her from deviating away from answering my question. Whenever I asked her about my daughter, Monique, she would change the subject. Monique had recently turned sixteen, and I was concerned about her, considering she hadn't been up to see me with my sister and mother in a minute. Finally, with enough probing from my part, I got my sister, Evelyn, to tell me what was going on.

When I hung up the telephone, twenty minutes later after talking with Evelyn, my head was spinning. My breaths were becoming very short as I forced myself to inhale and exhale. My legs were molten lead as I dragged myself back to the cell. During the course of walking, I vaguely heard people talking to me, but it seemed so far away. My mind was racing as I tried to digest the madness Evelyn had told me. By the time I reached my area and entered into the cell, I was perspiring profusely. I slowly sat down on the thin mattress and stared at the wall in front of me.

My daughter, my firstborn, had decided she wanted to live on her own. My mother had been trying to reprimand her for staying out late several weeks ago and seeing young men. My daughter became belligerent and ran out of the house.

My family hadn't heard from her. But yesterday, my sister told me she called and said that she was staying with a friend, and that she was okay. What had I done? Had I failed her? I'd unconsciously became an absentee father by being wrongfully imprisoned, and my daughter, a young black female, was seeking some form of guidance and comfort in a male father figure. She was probably confiding in this unknown man as he manipulated her into doing things that were not within her character. The system caused me to lose my child to the streets. I'd lost my baby girl to a vicious world out there, and I wasn't there for her—to protect her. I'd become the father I'd swore I never would be, and it was something that had been forcibly taken out of my hand.

When I'd been first accused of the crime of murder, I refused to submit to my emotions when the jury of my peers erroneously convicted me of a crime I didn't commit. I said to myself I'd be damned if they see me fall to my knees and beg them for mercy for something I didn't do. My father's blood is in me. Yet at that moment, all the flood gates opened, and I began to cry. I wasn't crying for all the horrible things that had happened to me. I was crying because I lost my daughter. I was crying because there was nothing I could do at that moment to reach out and take her in my arms and hug her. I was crying because I was a man whose livelihood had been stolen for no other reason than clearing the statistical books of some precinct commander who wanted to close a case on a murder that they had no answers for except by maliciously framing me. I cried, yes, I did. And through my tears, my strength was magnified. I'd be damned if I'd spend the next twenty years in a black hole while my family needed me on the outside. No, that picture wasn't in my future. I wiped away my tears, cleared my vision, and reached for my writing pad. Either I was going to write my way out of prison by convincing someone to believe me, or I was going to claw my way out by digging through law books and show I'd been given a raw deal in regard to an injustice, but one thing was certain, I would never sit down and accept my fate. *Never*!

I would have been at Comstock for two years when my counselor called me into his office one early afternoon to tell me that my transfer to another prison had been approved. He advised me to keep my nose clean, and within six months, I should be out of here.

I was waiting for my escort to return me back to the housing block that I was confined to. As I sat in the administration area of the prison, I was reading a book titled *The Art of War* when I looked up at the sound of shuffling feet to see three COs walking along side of a shackled inmate. He was being escorted to his counselor's office as well. Our eyes met. He had dark eyes with pale skin. He was a short, rotund man with black hair. He sat down beside a counselor's door several feet away as his three escorts stood beside him. As if on cue, the counselor's office door opened and he stuck his head out.

"Hello, David, come inside," the counselor said.

The man with the beady black eyes stood up and went inside his counselor's office.

When he disappeared, I suddenly remembered the face. I've always had a niche for remembering faces. And that niche had improved since my incarceration. His name was David Berkowitz, Son of Sam. Prison had its own celebrities, I thought. I watched as my escort appeared. He appeared to be in a rush, so I stood up and walked halfway to keep things short so he wouldn't complain.

A few days later, I was standing in front of the cell bars as they slowly opened to let me out to go to the yard for recreation. It was a summer night that was blistering with an unbearable humidity. It was too hot to be inside. I telephoned my family early that day about my transfer. My mother was extremely happy. The long trip to see me every two weeks was wearing her down. She was getting up in age, and I had to take that into consideration when I applied for my transfer.

By the time I reached the yard, it was full of people walking around with their shirts off trying to take advantage of the cool breeze that came by once in a while. I saw Critter on the basketball court, playing a five-man game. He was losing because every time someone on the other team made a point, he'd throw the ball against the fence. He was never a good player any way,

I thought. I stood there watching the game when the last shot from the opposition went into the basket. Critter screamed out a barrage of profanities. I walked over to him as he slid down to the ground.

"Bastards cheated," Critter said as I came closer.

"Just out of curiosity, how do you cheat in a basketball game when you're playing?" I asked as I stood over him, looking down.

"Uh-huh. I think Hector threw the game," Critter began as he tossed his head in the direction of a small, caramel-skinned Dominican walking out of the yard. "I had a box of cigarettes on this game."

"You don't smoke," I said. "And how do you know he threw the game?"

"Hector can shoot the ball, Shan. I've seen him shoot three pointers from midcourt. Now suddenly, the little snake is missing layups. And I don't smoke, but cigarettes buy my food. No, man, he threw the game, and if I find out, I'm going to—"

"They approved my transfer today," I said to cut him off. "It's at Green Haven and it's closer to the city."

Critter turned toward me. "Yeah, you're leaving?" I watched him bite his bottom lip, he was thinking. I'd been with him long enough to know his quirks. "I hear Green Haven is a laid-back prison," he said.

"So they say. They have a little more space to get around down there. You're up for your transfer in six months. Where are you going?" I asked.

Critter looked at me. "I don't know," he said.

"What about Green Haven?" I suggested.

"Man. I've been with you long enough. I might need a different scenery."

"Okay, cool. Where are you going?" I persisted.

"I haven't decided yet. I'll think of something," Critter said. "But for now, how is the situation going with Sal?"

"Sal is a paranoid-schizoid. I read the minutes of his trial, and some of the legal arguments his attorney raised on appeal were not preserved as a matter of trial transcript. I filed a State habeas corpus for him pro-se."

"You're going to Green Haven, huh?" Critter said.

I looked at him.

He shrugged.

"Think about it," I said.

He shrugged.

Stormville, New York, is where Green Haven was located. I had to go through the preliminary strip search and orientation process that lasted for five hours. Going from one prison to the next was demeaning to a human being. I hated it. My personal belongings would follow me later that day. As I stood among fifteen other men, facing the lieutenant as he walked up and down the line, making his point of authority by telling the new arrivals what was expected of us. I'd heard the greeting before as I stood there listening to the tall man. Another white man feeling a sense of power simply because he had control over others' fate. I realized that if a person is given a position of power to do as they willed, it was never a good thing for those who'd feel the lash of that power.

"My name is Lieutenant Blakely. I understand most of you men are coming from Attica, Clinton, Comstock, or other maximum security prisons. Here in Green Haven, we do things differently. This facility is run to accommodate you to a limit, yet all rules are to be adhered to at all times. Do I make myself clear?"

No one said a word.

"I guess we understand each other," Lieutenant Blakely said.

No one said a word.

"Welcome to Green Haven," Lieutenant Blakely said, as he turned and walked away.

Three days later, I was walking through the yard that afternoon, trying to get a feel of the new prison. Walking the yard, I saw that there appeared to be a laid-back atmosphere. When you do time, your body picks up on the slightest tension. I saw that there was a friendly mingling amongst the different races, and that was good. I saw a few people who'd I'd been doing time with walk by and give me either a nod or a handshake. Going to a new prison can be a little frightening because there is an unknown presence of not knowing what could happen or what you were walking into.

"Shan?" I turned to my left at the sound of my name. I saw a dark-skinned man waving at me on the other side of the yard. I couldn't make out and recognize the face at first. Was it someone I know from Albany Projects? Or from Comstock? I watched as the man approached.

"Shan?"

The man came closer. When I saw him, I knew who it was. It was Ronald. I'd met him in Downstate. He was an older brother. I recognized his salt-and-pepper hair. He lived in Newburgh, New York. He was an old pimp who didn't know when to let woman go and get legit.

"What's up, Ronald?" I said. "How long you been here?"

Ronald walked up to me and shook my hand. He was smiling. I looked down at his feet. He was wearing a pair of apple-green colored alligator shoes. He matched that with a green shirt. He was looking smooth. He had two gold teeth in the front of his mouth. His curly black hair and high yellow skin probably had women going crazy over him, I thought.

"What's up? Man, when did you get here?" Ronald asked. "Come on, let's walk the yard."

I nodded as I walked beside Ronald. Ronald was somewhat of a revered inmate. He'd been doing time since seventy-nine. He was a celebrity in every prison he went to. When he was arrested, the police said that he'd been running a multimillion dollar sex ring involving six states. He had police and judges on his payroll. I didn't see how selling sex could be so profitable, but he did it and sent away a few powerful men when he was caught. Ronald wasn't considered a snitch in the eyes of hustling. He was a negotiator who saw what they were trying to do to him in court and let the eggs fall where they lay. They were offering him one hundred years when he'd been arrested, but six months later, he began letting it be known that he would take down all the politicians in Newburgh as well as Albany if he didn't get a better deal. Those that didn't believe his threats were the ones he put the finger on. Now, years later, Ronald was looking at two or three more years before he would see the parole board. He was the type of man who told you like it was, and if you didn't like it, he didn't care. His temper was as fast and sharp as his wit. He'd enlightened me to a lot of things surrounding prison when we met in Downstate. He could be funny and vicious at the same time.

"I'm going to lay this knowledge on you, Shan, because you're all right with me, and I like how you carry yourself. Green Haven is a prison with opportunities if you're into that shit. It's like any other prison—to a point. You got your gamblers who are always sitting at one of those tables to the right of us for most of the day. You have your inmate politicians who are the elders, and they basically run the prison. There are many high profile prisoners here who are serving a life sentence and those who are just here. They have no sense of direction. The time is just doing them. Those guys you just stay away from because they are bound for destruction in an environment like this. The COs in here have their flaws also. There is one named Tersky who is trying to be someone important by making a name for himself by violating the rights of prisoners through abuse and assaults with his punk ass. He waits until you're handcuffed or there are five other COs with him. There are a few like him, but he's the king snake, always watch him. I don't have any trouble with any of them. You know how I walk, so I don't worry about a cracker like that or any man in here trying to make a name for themselves by targeting me," Ronald said.

I watched Ronald stealthily look around. He raised the front of his shirt. I saw a shank made of hard plastic tucked tightly in his waist. He dropped his shirt and glanced at me.

"You need a shank?" Ronald asked.

"No, Ro," I said. "I'm fighting to get out of here, not stay here, I'm good."

"This isn't like some of the other prisons I've been in. Dudes in here just want to drink homemade shine, get high, or get some ass from their wives on trailer visits or their girlfriends in the visiting room. Yet you still keep your eyes open in here, Shan. I don't care how easy it looks. It's still prison, man. Never get comfortable in any prison. If you do, then you've lost your edge to survive, and if you're lost, then you'd be walking around here like these other fools, thinking prison is nothing but doing time. Why do you think you have some of these idiots doing forty and fifty years after they'd done five or ten years previously? Because they got caught up in their own lies that they can do time no matter what. Any man can do time, but it's the man who takes that time and builds on it by returning back to his family and community as a productive member of his or her society. There are men in prison and there are little boys trying to act like men. You'll know which is which. Hey, how's Sherry? She's still hanging with you? She was a beautiful, young Philly."

I sighed. I'd forgotten Ronald and I used to talk while in Downstate. He was a good sounding board. "No, she went on about her business awhile back," I said. "When we were on the visit together that time and I saw her, I told you that she did not have the heart to do time. She was too damn pretty to be locked up. What did she say? 'It's too hard for me.' Or something like that."

"You know if you need to get pulled down to the visiting room and get your mind right, let me know. I'm locked up, but my ladies still take care of big daddy just like they're supposed to," Ronald said with a grin. "I'll let you know, but right now, freedom is the only thing on my mind, but thanks for the offer," I said.

"No problem, bro. Hey, let me cut the string. I have a few patsies I'm dealing with over in A-Block, and I see them now. Shan, I'm in B-Block if you need me."

I watched Ronald hurry away. He has walking with his pimp walk of kicking out the left leg smoothly and his right shoulder dipped downward rhythmically. Ronald was a hard man.

I walked the yard until it was time to go in for that afternoon. I had to get focused on how the new prison would be. If it was free as Ronald had mentioned, then maybe, I could really get into my writings.

It didn't take long for the program review to recommend that I be given a mess hall job. At first, I was hesitant, but after the first three days, I saw how the inmates were working the mess hall. The mess hall was a gold mine. Inmates bought everything from eggs, flour, sugar, or anything that could be sold. Yeast, potato skins, and sugar sold quickly. These items in question were bought to make wine. It could be done in a few days of mixing everything and letting it sit to ferment for a few days. Working in the mess hall, I became appreciative of making my own food. At least, I knew what I was eating.

Eight months later, I had to admit, Ronald had told me right about Green Haven being a prison that allows you to run loose. The prison let you do your own time. There were a lot of programs that were geared to anything you thought might help you do your time easier—at least, I first thought. I decided to enroll in the Black Studies programs as well as "The Resurrection Study Group" that teaches the nontraditional approach to criminal and social justice. I found out later that this class was founded and taught by two of the most powerful black men in the entire prison system. They both were from the Black Panther Party and perhaps the smartest men I have ever spoken to. Eddie Ellis and Larry Lukeman White, between the both of them, they had nearly fifty years in. They both came to prison in the early seventies. It was because of these two men that I began to understand the plight of Africans here in America. They taught young black men that just because you were in prison does not excuse you from your obligation to the betterment of black people. That being responsible to your family and community is expected if you were to remain in their study group. I became a full-fledged member and study I did.

I continued my education and enrolled in the prison Youth Assistant Program (YAP). This was a program that was first hard to get clearance for due to the interaction with trouble kids from surrounding counties that the courts or other agencies felt needed harsh reality counseling. I excelled so well in this program that I became the Director in one year. I learned that I had very good moderating skills and group dynamics strategies that these kids identified with. I knew that every kid that came into that visiting room for a session with my YAP Counselors had troubled lives and was pleading for help and I knew that I had to do all that I could to save them. I knew at that point that their fight became mine. After what happened to me, I had a passion for change.

After dinner, most inmates were either going to college or to their programs for the evening. Green Haven's policy was a simple one. Get educated or get a hands-on skill or get the hell out of that prison. The administration did not accept inmates doing nothing at Green Haven.

I sat in the middle of the room in Black Studies. I was surprised that there were actually twelve other men sitting in there with their pens and pads ready to take notes. The room had pictures of black leaders, both male and female, on the walls. I was never one of those who didn't have a grasp of my cultural history, considering my father had his militant ways woven into my mind as a child early on, but sitting here in this class, I became proud of knowing that men of color weren't simply slaves forcibly brought over to North America to make it blossom with their sweat, blood, and tears, but they'd been proud leaders in dark continents around the world for thousands of years. They'd been scientists, explorers, doctors, intellectuals, and many others. My pride as a black man exploded. As a child growing up in public school, I'd been taught—no, I'd been brainwashed by the public school educational system that the black man contributed nothing of significance to the world, and as I sat in class learning my black culture, I realized that whomever owned the media and books of education, own the minds of those receiving that education. I had been one of those lost souls of color once, but now I was opening my mind to a society that frowns on those with dark skin. I was looking at the world through pristine eyes while learning history at that moment, and it was a world that had many flaws in it. My false imprisonment was proof of that.

My life being snatched away without one iota of truth spoke volumes when it came to seeing the truth. I would eventually drink in greedily the teachings of my Black Studies classes and apply it to my everyday existence in prison. I had begun to find my strength, and I'd be damn if I let anyone redirect my cause to continue to get strong. I had everything to lose if I didn't confront a system that had wronged me, just like it had wronged hundreds or thousands of others before me.

A light in my head to educate myself went off, and I could not turn it out. I became obsessed with learning. I read all books: science, psychology, history, and most of all, law books. I realized that I would not be able to help myself if I did not know how the system works. If I could understand the dynamics that fuel the system and how it allowed for injustices to occur, then I could fight back and education will be my armor.

𝕴𝖓𝖍𝖆𝖑𝖎𝖓𝖌 𝕯𝖊𝖊𝖕𝖑𝖞

(Autumn and Spring 1990-1993)

It was in the middle of the year when I looked on the roster sheet of inmates arriving to the prison. A smile came to my face when I saw a name I didn't think I'd see again.

"Faison? Put the paper down and get to your post."

I didn't have to look up to know who that irritating voice belonged to.

"Come on! Get to your position!"

I stood up while placing the inmate movement sheet on the table to the right of me. I didn't do this quickly in hopes that the man speaking to me would know that I didn't jump to his beck and call.

"Do you need a write up, Faison?"

I stopped and stared at the pale man standing a few feet from me. It was my way of letting him know he couldn't intimidate me, I knew his kind. They wanted you to bow down to their demands and smile in their face like a shuffling imbecile. I'd seen a few inmates go through the scenario whenever he came around. I refused to let him think that he could do that to me.

"CO Tersky, you are aware of the ten-minute break we get after completing one of our tasks, aren't you?" I asked.

The pale man rolled his eyes while swirling his nightstick. "Faison, save the rule crap and get to work," Tersky said.

I stared at him.

"Save the stares for later, Faison. Get to your position."

This man probably used to get bullied as a kid, I thought, as I stared at him. Men like him were weak in their lives, and when they're given an opportunity to make other people's lives miserable, they jump on it. I knew men like him. They were molded from nothing great in life but gave hell simply because they could.

"You ever think about taking the test to become a lieutenant, Tersky?" I asked, as I began slowly walking.

"For what? To be kissing everyone who has authority ass? No. I like my job right here," he said, as he continued to swirl his nightstick.

"You like thinking you're the boss, huh?" I asked.

"I am the boss of you and all these other degenerates. So why would I give all this up to walk around with my head up my ass as a lieutenant? There's no fun in that."

I stared hard at him. He returned my stare while still swinging his nightstick. I huffed with discontent as I continued to walk by him. Tersky would never give up his position. He loved being in charge and giving orders to those who couldn't resist his authoritative dictatorship. He was a little man with a big head who lived on his ego.

By the time I reached my designated area, which was the bread area, Scott, a middle-aged Irish man, was pouring flour into a large, flat pan. "What's up, Scott?" I said as I wrapped a hairnet around my head and hurried over to assist him. "Sorry I was late getting back. Tersky held me up." "Tersky is a dickhead. Don't worry about it. Lather up those pans with butter. How are things going with your appeal?" Scott said.

I began putting butter in the seven pans that were lined up on a metal table to the left of me. "Some men don't know how to handle a little bit of power," I said.

Scott had a wicked sense of humor. He was from Schenectady, New York. He had a long scar running down from the right side of his face. It started at the top of his head and ran down his chin. His was brawny with a cool demeanor. We'd been working together from the first day we both started in the mess hall.

"They denied my appeal for retrial for lack of any reversible legal argument. The appellate court said that I was given due process of the law, and my sentence fell within the guidelines of that conviction," I said. "Also, since none of the appellate court judges that heard my appeal had a dissenting opinion, the Court of Appeals will not issue a certificate to appeal before their court."

"Okay, so the total of their explanation boils down to bull and more bull, right?" Scott asked.

"Yeah," I said.

"Don't let it stop you from filing another appeal. Keep researching your case and find that legal argument that will compel the appellate court to hear your appeal."

"You're right, Scott. I just have to keep it going on a different front," I said.

"Me, I've been through three appeals already, and why should I stop filing motions just because they say my confession was the apple on the table. Hell, I was so drunk that night when I killed my girl friend, I don't remember doing it. Now if I don't remember that, how can you say that I confessed to killing her? I've been fighting that for ten years now and will keep fighting it until things go in my favor, or I wake up one morning to old to file a motion."

"Don't give up the fight, man," I said.

"And neither should you," Scott said. "Let me get those pans. The dough is ready."

I gave him two pans.

Later that evening, I was waiting in the yard. The new arrivals had been processed by that time. I was standing off to the side, just observing as I watched a familiar face appear in the doorway.

"Critter," I shouted as I made my way toward him.

I watched Critter walk towards me. He was smiling.

"So you made it to the new spot, huh?" I asked as we shook hands. "I thought you weren't coming."

"What the hell. One prison is no different than the next," Critter said as he looked around. "I don't feel the tension like in Comstock though."

"I know, and here, they don't scrutinize you with a microscope," I said.

"How are you coming along with your letter writing?" Critter asked.

"It's good. I created a journal so I can date and name the people I've sent out letters to. If they respond to me, then I place a star next to their name and continue writing them, if no one writes me back, I place a green mark next to their name and I write them again. I do not accept any non-favorable answers," I said.

"That sounds good. Have you heard from Mathematics since his parole?" Critter asked.

I'd forgotten about that. "Man, Mathematics went out in the streets of Brooklyn in the Marcy Projects with that attitude of his, and some young boys put six bullets in him. Math is dead," I said it with painful remorse. I felt guilty because I couldn't change Mathematics's outlook on life. He was a wild one who wouldn't change. "I heard he had a nice funeral though."

"Mathematics was a hot head, Shan. No matter how many times he was told to calm his attitude, he still did what he wanted to do. I hope you're not carrying the weight of that on your shoulders. Even though he was from your old neighborhood does not make you liable for his short fall," Critter said. "You tried."

"Yeah, I guess."

"Shan, we can't carry the burdens of others on our shoulders. It gets too heavy and drags you down. Let this one go, man."

Critter was right. I tried to guide Mathematics away from the wilderness and into something positive, but he didn't want that. He had great parents, and his mother loved him completely. You see how she used to come see him every two weeks like clockwork for years. I can imagine how devastated she was from his death.

"Anyway, come to the mess hall when they ask you what program you want. We can eat anything we want in there," I said.

"If I go there, I don't have to spend much money in commissary," Critter commented, as he contemplated his choice. "Saving a few dollars does make a difference."

"That's right."

Critter looked at me. Simultaneously, we started laughing.

After working in the mess hall for two weeks with Critter, I knew the first week that working in the kitchen wasn't his forte. Every time I turned around, he was either making some personal food like cakes, pies, steaks, skinless chicken, or anything that met his fancy. To him, the mess hall had become his private kitchen.

The day things hit the fan was when Critter told CO Tersky that he'd rather eat rattle snake than work for his redneck, incest breed, idiot. Yes, that got him placed in keep-lock, meaning he was locked in his cell twenty-three hours a day until he went in front of a lieutenant to straighten out his write-up.

I went to see him in his cell two days later. Considering I had been voted in to be on the grievance committee, I could walk throughout the prison, assisting inmates in researching and filing grievances. My writing skills had made a name for me throughout the prison. Being a grievance representative gave me unlimited access to the prison population. Critter was sitting on the bed when I arrived.

"You had to curse Tersky out, huh? You couldn't ignore him like everyone else, could you?" I asked.

Critter looked at me.

"Critter, you have to be careful messing with these COs in here, man. These mountain climbers up here could make you disappear if you act too crazy. I brought you some food."

Critter stood up and took the plate of food. "So what do you think the disciplinary board might give me for cursing out Tersky?" he asked.

"Maybe fifteen or twenty days in keep-lock if you don't curse out the lieutenant during your hearing," I said with a smirk.

"They can kiss my ass," Critter said. "Can I file a grievance on him?"

"For what? You cursed him out and he has some snitches that'll vouch for him that you called him other names as well. No, that won't work," I said as I shook my head and smiled. "You're going to have to be cool with your temper."

"All right, I guess I'll be cooling my feet in keep-lock for a while," Critter said.

I laughed. "I will stop by and bring you food until you get out. I have to make some stops over in G-Block to hear some grievances," I said.

"Well, see me tomorrow," Critter said, as I watched him stuff his mouth with food.

"Okay," I said as I walked away.

The next day, I was walking in to the visiting room to see my mother, sister, and son. He was almost four years old and very verbal. I hugged them all before sitting down. I picked up my son and put him on my knee.

"Ma, how was the ride on the bus?" I asked as I watched my mother sip from a can of apple juice.

"Not bad at all, much shorter ride than Comstock that's for sure," Mom said.

I bounced Antwan on my knee as he laughed and tried to pull my lips. He was taking on the facial features of his mother, I noticed. I glanced at my sister, Evelyn. It looked like she was trying to avoid my eyes.

"How is work, Evelyn?" I asked. I knew she was now a teacher working in a Montessori School in Downtown Brooklyn. I was so very proud of her.

She looked at me.

"What's wrong?" I asked. I guess she noticed the concern in my voice because she straightened her back and exhaled.

"I'm getting married," Evelyn said very quickly.

My mouth dropped.

"Anthony, she isn't a little girl."

"Let her have her day," Mom said.

I looked at their faces. All I could see was affection for a man I'd never met but who was marrying my sister. He must be a good man because my mother was indirectly giving her support. I decided to change the subject.

"What's going on with Monique?" I asked.

My mother's face became hardened. "I have tried to talk to Monique, and each time that I do, she feels I'm intruding in her life, Anthony. She is sixteen going on fifty. She is messing around with a man twenty-five years old, and I hear they're living together," she said.

My heart felt heavy in my chest and the rage I felt for this man bedding my sixteen-year-old daughter engulfed me. Knowing that this man was committing statutory rape on my daughter had me thinking the most dangerous thoughts.

"Anthony, she is stubborn. We tried to guide her, but every time we tried to discipline her, she'd disappear for days," Evelyn said. "She's an old soul who wants to do her own thing."

I was a father with no voice as to the rearing of my child. I felt inept even to the point of trying to tell my family how to confront my child. At this point and by the dispositions my mother and sister were displaying, I knew that any act against her would be fruitless. I handed my son to my sister and stood up.

"Evelyn, you have my blessing to marry. I'm good with it. Can I meet him before you marry him?" I asked. My voice was empty. I was exhausted. "I hope you'll give me that opportunity."

Evelyn stared at me. I watched as tears began to form in the corner of her doe-like eyes. She smiled as she nodded her agreement.

I turned around and headed toward the exit. I'd ended my visit with my family early. At that moment, I felt as if I wanted to go hide under a large rock and never come out from under it. Useless is a powerful feeling. It takes away the very essence of a man, and that's how I was feeling. It was a feeling of grasping for unreachable entities that you can never really grab. My daughter's way of life at such a young age had hit me hard. I was a father with no say-so as to her actions and how they could be detrimental to her. No emotional guidance to make her stronger to endure the pains that life had for her. I was feeling more and less of a father with each passing day. At this stage in my life, I was feeling more like a sperm donor than a man who swore he'd die for his daughter on the day she was born. I was empty, and no one could help me find solace…no one.

Some people come to prison and pray for forgiveness. They even find salvation by praying every day and becoming new Christians. But what did I have to pray for? I'd done nothing to warrant prison and fighting for my life to get out of it! Do I denounce God and swear to the world that I'd been falsely accused of committing a crime I hadn't done? Do I pick up a knife and begin killing anyone who gets in my way as I try to break out? Do I sit on the edge of my bed one late night playing with entwined sheets, contemplating where I should tie them while make a noose to hang myself? So many intangibles but very few answers.

I knew as I took that painful stroll back to that lonely cell that God wouldn't save me or let the world know there was a man sitting in prison rotting for no other reason than someone not wanting to find the truth. I knew that I, Anthony Faison, would have to find a way to beat a judicial system that had thought it had strangled me with its legal injustice, its misrepresentation of equality. No, the greatest words I'd ever read while reading the Bible my first year of imprisonment was the purest of words I'd ever read: *"God helps those who help themselves."*

Critter and I had becomes friends as the years wore on. I could talk to him, and he could relay his crazy thoughts to me whenever he felt like talking, which was very little at times, but he was a great sounding board. He'd finally decided to go to the barber shop as a program requirement. The man couldn't cut hair with a lawn mower, but who was I to tell him he couldn't. People who entered the barber shop for a haircut would go around him, so he wouldn't ask them if they needed a haircut. The first three months even I avoided him when it came to getting my hair cut. The man was atrocious with clippers and a pair of scissors. But this day was different. It was a pre-special day.

As I sat in Critter's barber chair that afternoon, I had to avoid the eyes of other men looking at me as if I'd lost my mind for sitting in Critter's chair. I tensed as Critter placed the barber's wrap around my neck and secured it with a pin. I was facing the mirror and looking at Critter through it.

"So how do you want me to cut it?" Critter asked. I got scared!

"Man, I want you to cut it so it looks good," I responded defensively. "Fade me out on the sides and give me a tapper fade in the back." I continued to stare with apprehension as Critter took out the clippers from the box on the counter in front of me. "I don't want it too low either."

"No problem. I will give you a two on the top and a one on the sides," Critter said as he hit the power switch on the clippers in his hand. "Then I'd get the split ends on the top afterward."

I felt myself tense as Critter brought the hair clippers toward my hair.

"You're going to your first parole hearing tomorrow, huh?" I said.

The hair clippers stopped in midair.

"Yeah, but I'm not looking forward to seeing the streets anytime soon. I'm bringing them seven and a half years with no education and no certificates of purpose, so I'm figuring on getting hit with two more years," Critter said as he came around and stood in front of me.

"You don't know that for sure, my friend. The parole board has been letting a lot of people go home these past three months. This might be your shot," I said, as I glanced at what the hell Critter was doing to my hair.

I watched Critter nod. "It's been a long time since I've been in those streets, Shan. They've changed."

"I know you're not trying to tell me you're scared. Look around you, man. What man wouldn't kill to have the opportunity that you're having tomorrow, huh? Critter, you survived this long because you carried yourself like a man and people respected you as a man. You know how this prison life is. If a person thinks you can be punked, you get punked. A lot of brothers around here respect you, and for that, you'd be surprised how many are hoping you do make that first board, then they'd know they have a shot of making it as well. Get in there and sell yourself for some freedom," I said.

I watched Critter as he turned the hair clippers on and off while thinking.

"You know, Shan, you're right," Critter said as he walked around to the back of the chair.

I watched Critter comb my hair in preparation to cut it. I closed my eyes as I heard the clippers slowly begin their descent toward my hair—Lord, help me.

"Shan, what's up?"

I opened my eyes to see Beatty walking through the door. He was another barber and better than Critter.

I leaped out of the chair while snatching off the barber's cape.

"Beatty!" I shouted with delight as I gave Critter his barber's cape. "I was waiting for you."

"Shan, what happened to your cut?" Critter asked.

"I'll let you cut me next week," I said as I literally ran to Beatty's barber chair and jumped into it before someone beat me to it.

"You have no faith in my professionalism, Shan," Critter said. "I'm hurt."

"I believe in your barbering skills. Trust me, I do."

Beatty looked at me. "Why didn't you let Critter cut your hair?" he asked.

"You know Critter," I said. "Plus Critter can be a little reckless with those hair clippers. I saw him cut a brother's hair last week, and the man's hairline was pushed back farther. So when I told him, he told me that Critter told him his hairline was that way before he'd sat in his chair."

"Maybe it was," Beatty said, as I watched him place the barber's cape around my neck. "Some of these brothers do have more to work with than they think when they sit in a barber's chair."

"Beatty, the man said that Critter has been telling him that for the past three months! Every time he gets out of the chair, his hairline is farther back than before," I said.

Beatty and I glanced over at Critter who was trying to coerce someone into his barber's chair as he snipped his scissors in the air while turning his hair clippers on and off rhythmically.

We said in unison, "Critter can be extreme when it comes to cutting hair."

We both laughed.

I was right in making the call about Critter being paroled. He made his first parole board. I was happy for him. He was a good dude and loyal. I asked him to meet me in the law library later that evening.

After dinner, I asked to be let out of my cell to go assist someone with a grievance. By seven o'clock, I was sitting a few feet away from the door as I waited for Critter. I didn't know what I wanted to talk to him about, but there was that feeling of being near someone who was going home that gave me a new drive to seek out my freedom desperately. I watched as Critter walked in with his Harlem jaunt. He saw me and walked over.

"What's up, Shan?" Critter asked as he sat down across from me.

I stared at him. I would miss Critter. Not for any other reason than he was a good listener and gave good advice. It is difficult to find people in prison who you could trust and feel a sense of respect for. Critter was that person.

"Yeah, I wanted to talk to you about hitting those bricks in the next two months. I don't want to see you back in here talking about how it's hard out there in the streets. You're more than that, man. Don't get caught out there trying to catch up to time you've lost already, and please, bro, don't catch one of those young chicken heads and get her pregnant."

Critter smiled.

"I'm serious, man. You got through this time by keeping your head straight and clear, don't get in those streets and lose your direction. If you come back in here and I see you, I will bust you in the head with a dumbbell as soon as I see you in the yard." He knew I was kidding, but saying it gave us both an inside laugh.

We stared at each other for a full minute. Neither one of us said a word. I didn't know if Critter was taking my advice critically or personally. He was always a hard poker player to read whenever I asked him something.

Critter cleared his throat. "Shan, man, I love you like a brother. I won't let the streets corrupt me and find myself back in this place. You definitely will never see me doing this again, and you can depend on me to take care of things in the street if you need me," he said.

"All I ask is that you don't forget about a brother when you smell that concrete. Don't let me receive a 'return to sender' letter when I write you," I said.

Critter laughed. "No, man, I will write back. Let me know what you need. Well, not immediately. You know I have to get a job and start making money. You know it will be hard to get it together after seven years in here. But I'm not going anywhere."

Words can be that at times, but as I watched Critter, I knew he was telling me the truth. He wasn't going anywhere or wouldn't forget about me. He was a real friend. You know you have a real friend in your life when no matter what the situation might be, they are there for you, and you are there for them. In prison, you don't make too many friends, but the ones you do make, stay with you to the end.

"I'm going to miss you, man," I said.

"Man, don't. I'm with you in spirit," Critter said.

It would be August 1993 when I would see the last of Critter.

The Painful Years

(1994-1999)

Prison has a way of bringing time to a standstill. I began to really concentrate on my education. Ten months after Critter had been released, I got a letter from him telling me he was getting married. I laughed. Who would want to marry a crazy man like him? I was wrong. Critter was a good person. Probably some woman caught sight of that and snatched him up. I told my mother about Critter getting married, and she was happy for him. He, my sister, and my mother were in touch with each other in the street. Critter was like family to me now. You don't meet many brothers like that inside, and he was a brother that was trusted and loyal. A man whom I could count on no matter what. When he sent me pictures of his wife and their wedding, I was dumbfounded. I showed his pictures to most of the prison, and everyone that saw them respected him even more for changing his life. I was proud of him and wrote him telling him exactly that.

I'd met a guy by the name of Roth about a year after Critter had left. He was from Brownsville, Brooklyn. He was a tall, thin, caramel-complexioned brother who wore thick glasses. He'd been doing his bid since ninety-one. It was his first bid, and I thought he didn't respect it. In his mind, he believed himself to be smarter than anyone. Roth was a hustler to the fullest extent of the word. He didn't care how or who he hustled. That attitude is cool in the street, but in prison, it is deadly. Roth was getting heroin on consignment from a couple of Columbian dealers on the other side of the prison. I'd told him on numerous occasions that his thirst for getting high would get him in trouble one day. He never listened. You can only tell people where their actions might lead, but you can't direct them if they refuse to be helped. Roth thought he could smile and grin his way into his dealer's heart, but a dealer, regardless of where he might be, was a man trying to make money and not friends. Roth was a good dude, but he liked getting high, and in prison, you shouldn't have any weaknesses, especially those weaknesses when you depend on others to help feed that monkey. Roth had let his need become someone else's greed.

My codefendant, Chris, was transferred to Green Haven. It is a rarity when two codefendants are in the same prison. Our relationship had deteriorated over the years. I'd heard stories about Chris from other inmates who knew we were codefendants. He was going around telling people that he was in prison because of me. I was flabbergasted when I heard about this. My first act was to really go at him hard for creating that terrible rumor, but I didn't want to create any bad vibes between us. But how could he say something so gut wrenching about me? Neither one of us committed the crime, so why would he say things like that? I was angry. I knew I had to corner him somewhere and get the truth from him. I had to hear from his own lips as to why he was saying these horrific things about me. I decided to confront him a few days later in the yard.

I approached Chris with a lot of anger and bad intentions in my heart as I walked toward him. He was waiting for me near one of the many televisions near the east side. He was surrounded by a few guys we both knew from Brooklyn. I could tell all eyes fell on me when I approached. He'd probably been telling them the same story, I thought.

"Hey, Chris, let me talk to you for a minute," I said.

Chris looked around at the guys standing around him. Chris had never been a man who could think on his own. He needed others encouragement to make his decision. I'd known this since we were younger. He possessed that weakness about him that always made me cautious of him. He broke away from the crowd and followed me.

"Yo, man, why are you telling people I'm the reason you're in here?" I asked. I had to pace my words carefully so that I didn't lash out at him. "You know we're both in here for something we didn't do. What's wrong with you saying things like that?"

Chris kept walking while playing with his fingernails. He didn't respond.

"Did you hear what I said?" I asked.

"I didn't say anything like that," Chris said.

I glanced at him. I knew him. He was lying. He didn't look at me, and that's how I knew he was lying.

"First off, neither one of us did this crime, and the fact that I got these men coming at me telling me that my codefendant is speaking negative about me is not right. Man, I'm in my cell every night writing letters to people, hoping someone will take our case and see our wrongful conviction plight and help us. I don't need my codefendant whispering behind my back, making me look silly!" I snapped.

"Man, I'm not saying anything about you, I don't know where that's coming from," Chris said. His words were short and crisp.

I stopped walking and stared at him. He stopped as well, but he still didn't look in my face. He continued to play with his fingernails.

He was lying.

"Whatever you're hearing, it's not coming from me," Chris said.

Who did this man think he was talking to? I asked myself. He was belittling my intelligence with his weak answers.

I had to walk away from him. If I didn't, I would've found myself punching him in the face, and I didn't want that tension between us; although it was there in the shadows of our conversation, he was still my codefendant and we had to have a unified front.

I had to limit my connection with Chris as we moved through Green Haven with the passing of time. I couldn't trust him. As such, I had to concentrate on school and continued my letter writings in hopes of someone responding to me.

One day in the summer of 1999, I was walking in the yard when I saw Roth running toward the CO's booth. I watched as two other men gave chase. Their faces were covered with sweat hoods, making their features difficult to see. Roth was fast, but one of his pursuers was faster. I watched as the lead chaser neared Roth within arm's length. I saw the man raise his left arm. In his hand was a shiny, metal object. He brought it down toward Roth. I saw Roth arch. When his pursuer pulled his arm away, I saw blood follow. I watched as Roth fell forward. Both pursuers were now on top of Roth as he lay facedown within seconds. They were both stabbing him repeatedly. Roth's screams were ear shattering as he begged for help. I was too far away to help him, and as I made an effort to trot toward him, his screams stopped. Yet that didn't stop his attackers as they continued to stab his lifeless body.

I heard the whistles blowing around the yard as the COs began running toward Roth and his attackers. Each attacker ran away as the COs hurriedly approached. With their matching sweat hoods, they blended into a crowd of people several feet away. I knew why they'd run into the crowd. Their act was common among inmates. As they blended into the crowd, they would take off their sweat hoods, and no one would know their identities. It was an illusionary trick to throw off the COs. It usually worked. They would never find out who stabbed Roth. It was life in prison, and if you became a statistic, no one cared. One inmate being murdered by another inmate meant nothing to the authorities. It was a day in the life behind the wall.

I had found myself staying in my cell with each passing month to write letters. You might even say that I'd become a cell hermit. My years in prison had shown me the most barbaric of men as well as those men who possess a sense of class in some instances. It's not the cage that turns a man into an animal; it's the mentality of the man that gets lost in the cage as he lets despair take a hold of him. I became withdrawn after the death of Roth. I had to find a shell to continue my struggle. An area of contemplation in which I didn't lose my mind and fall into a moral pit of debauchery in which I'd never climb out of. No one can teach you how to do time; time teaches you how to survive.

I was in the law library in the fall of that year. I'd been to see the doctor concerning the constant headaches I'd been having since the beginning of the year. The doctor gave me the usual prescription of aspirin after telling me it was probably stress. I laughed at him when I exited his small, back room office. What did I have to be stressful of? Would it be the fact that I was in prison confronting a judicial system that had taken away my life? Or the fact that I was surrounded by men who could laugh with you one moment and stab you the next for no particular reason?

When I was in the law library, I always watched the information board that had contact numbers and business cards of lawyers and ex-cops who were now doing private investigator work. For some reason, I was drawn to a card that had a man's name on it. There was nothing unusual about the name, mind you. I was just drawn to it. The name on the card was Michael Race. Maybe it was the last name that caught my eye. Race. *Like being in a race to get free*, I thought. I took the card. I went immediately to my cell. I grabbed my journal. I placed Michael Race's name in it as well as the time and date. I reached for my writing pad, and I began writing:

Dear Mr. Michael Race,

I'm sure you've probably heard this many times before and I probably won't be the last to say this to you, but I have been imprisoned for a crime I didn't do, and I would appreciate you taking up my cause to help me prove I didn't murder the man in which I'd been convicted. I am innocent, and I've written thousands of letters to many men and women, seeking assistance in proving my innocence. I have been wrongfully convicted and would like for you to be my investigator to prove my injustice.

The letter I'd written was from my heart. I felt like I was breathing into it with each letter that touched the paper. It had become an extension of my very soul. I felt that the letter was my hand reaching out to Mr. Race and compelling him to take my case. I'd written thousands of letters before, and I'd written them from my mind as I strategized my purpose and why I was writing them. Yet while writing to this man, it all seemed to flow with each breath I inhaled and exhaled. The letter had become alive, and I wanted it to reach out and touch him.

I noticed that my letter writing had become intense, regardless of whom I wrote to. I made it my business that the reader felt my passion. They had to feel that this particular letter was not just a standard letter from someone just talking but rather a letter from someone who had been wronged. I began to write as if I was obsessed and every letter fueled my drive.

At night, when all the other inmates had turned off their lights to sleep, my lights stayed on all night. I found the quiet of the night to be the most peaceful and the best time to formulate my thoughts on paper.

There were many nights when I was startled from the screams of men whose inner demons were attacking their souls. Who let out these horrific cries while they were asleep. Then there were those men who waited for everyone to fall asleep and then they would go to the back of their cells and cry in the darkness of the night. Through all this, I remained focused and prayed for their souls as I prayed for my own.

There were days when I would walk the yard and let my mind run free. My mother and sister had persuaded my daughter, Monique, to come visit me. She was twenty years old, but appeared much older than I'd expected her to be. I wanted to know what was going on in her life. It was a conversation that was short in essence. She didn't talk much. She listened without making much of a fanfare about it. She had an "I know what I'm doing" attitude that I really didn't appreciate, but what more could I say or do? I hadn't been in her life in years. She's become her own mother and father to survive in the streets. She'd been placed in foster care after refusing to return to school. My mother had told me that there was nothing she could do with her. I felt so useless as I sat there staring at my firstborn child. The little girl in her standing out as I tried to reprimand her without being overbearing. Yet in my heart, I wanted to grab her and shake her into reality. To let her know that I was in prison with the possibility of life, but I was still her father! The same man who bathed her, changed her, and fed her as a child. I wanted to say other things as well, but I didn't want to push her out of my life with any force. I needed her, and I knew she needed me, if for no other reason than to have the comfort of knowing that I was with her in spirit. She was my daughter and I loved her.

After an hour and a half of being silent, she began to open up to me. She wanted me home. She wanted me to take her shopping. She wanted me to meet her boyfriend. She wanted me to do so many things with her, and all I could say was that our time together would come, and that I was sorry I wasn't with her during her most crucial years of growing up. I couldn't get those years back, but I would make it up to her. She kissed me and told me she loved me. Just hearing her say those words made my heart swell with joy. Twenty minutes later, I watched as she exited the visiting room. A sadness gripped my throat. How much can you say to a twenty-year-old with so little bit of time on your side? I said what was in my heart, and I guess she knew it when she heard it.

All of this ran through my mind as I walked the yard. Two days previously, I held a good man in my arms as he died from an aneurism. I was still having night sweats about that experience. Clifford Wilson was his name, and he had been in prison twenty-five years when I met him. There'd been many days and nights when he and I had walked the yard, talking about everything and anything. He was very smart and he taught me a lot, and he did so by first giving me a book a week to read. An older man who was doing a life sentence for the murder of his wife in a jealous rage. I was surprised one day when he told me he was Flip Wilson's brother. I thought nothing of it. Some people come to prison and want to be other people in hopes that it would give them some personal prestige. I merely went along with him. He'd informed me that he and Flip Wilson had grown up together and how each had chose a different road for success. Clifford had taken the easy road by going into a life of crime, and his brother Flip had chosen laughter to get out of the ghetto. To confirm his words, he brought out pictures of them together during different eras of time. I have to say, I was impressed with the pictures. Clifford was a good man who'd died behind bars, but he always would tell me that he had no regrets about his life, as if trying to justify to me that he was content. To me, it didn't make a difference. I'd stopped judging people a very long time ago.

His death in my arms would stay with me with every waking day. I didn't want to die in prison. I didn't want to have a CO decide I'd done things egregious to him and attack me in my cell late at night. These things were a reality that could happen to me any day or at any given moment. Death lingered on me as well as any other person doing time.

I'd seen many killings in prison over the years. Some were totally senseless and without merit. When you have nothing but time on your hand, anything to make that time go quicker is a relief, so men become more sensitive to things they would've ignored in the street. A hard look could lead to a person getting their throat cut. A bump in the hallway while going to the mess hall could get a person jumped and beaten to the point of death. There were instances whereas another inmate stared too hard at a woman who had come to visit someone. That person would be in the hospital ward by the end of the day with multiple stab wounds throughout his body.

In prison, you learned fast that respect is everything, and if it does not concern you, mind your damn business.

After a long night of writing and as the sun began to rise, I noticed an eerie feeling in the air. Everything appeared to be delayed for some reason. I stood up and looked out the bars out into the prison yard. Out of the corner of the wall, I could vaguely see what appeared to be a lot of cars. I could hear the engines, but I thought nothing of it as I gathered all my mail to place in the outgoing box. I wanted to go to the mess hall for breakfast. When I returned and was walking down the corridor from the mess hall, I saw something that frightened me like nothing before. Now that I had a view to the front of the prison, I was able to see at least one hundred police cars from jurisdictions all over the state and they had literally surrounded the prison. Each car had on their blue and red lights.

I looked at Maleek and asked him what the hell is going on and that's when he told me that a cop killer was going to the parole board today and his name was Herman Bell. I learned from years of working in the law library and seeing that cop killers never make parole.

The Scent of Freedom

(Spring-Fall 2000-2001)

After ten straight years of being imprisoned at Green Haven, a prison that raised me mentally and provided the mental tools that I would need to fight the system that had stolen my life, I was transferred in the fall of 2000 to Dannemora Prison. It was two hours from Canada. I did the preliminary introduction when first arriving with the lieutenant like all the other prisons I'd been in. I'd become numb with it. I was taken to a new cell block and gradually began to fit in over the course of three weeks. The people in prison change, but prison always stays the same. You have breakfast, lunch, dinner, recreation time, or a program to attend, then visits. This is the continued structure of prison. To oppress you if you become too outspoken. To deny you the simplest wants and needs when most desired. It continuously reminded you that you're not human; you were subhuman with an animalistic craving to rebel against all things that were deemed productive in society. These same people judge you and sentence you all with one breath. Yet when you are innocent, you receive nothing. A cold shoulder and nothing more.

I had some good news to get me through the day. I'd heard from Michael Race. He wanted to see me. He said he wanted to look into my eyes rather than us corresponding with each other in letters. I was comfortable with that. I wanted him to see my face and hear my pain as we talked to one another. Leaving Green Haven was a relief. I'd grown tired of hearing how my codefendant was talking behind my back. There were stories he was concocting that were blatant lies, and each time I asked him about it, he'd say he wasn't saying anything about me. He was lying. As I struggled to get freedom, not only for me but him as well, he walks around the prison saying I was the reason he was in prison. I had come to the point that he was ignorant, and ignorance can never be changed, it had to be confronted. Chris was ignorant and more. Yet I had to blank him out altogether or else I might've lost my mind trying to understand him. He was as complicated as a rock sitting in a stream of water. We'd come to a point in which we'd stopped talking to each other for months, and things weren't getting any better between us, so the transfer was good in that way. I think if I'd stayed there any longer, he and I would've had to go at it, and I didn't want that.

A week later, I was sitting in the cell writing a letter when I heard the jingling of the CO keys walking down the tier. He stopped in front of the cell and said, "Faison, you have a legal visit. Put on state issues." As I hurried and dressed, I wondered who this could have been since I was not expecting anyone. As we entered into the administration building where the visiting rooms were located, I saw from a distance what looked like a cop. You know cops got this distinctive look about themselves.

I knew at that moment that it was Investigator Michael S. Race. He was about five feet ten in height, had a stocky build, and had a look like he knew what he was doing and in doing it, left no stone unturned.

As I approached, he stood and extended his hand and said, "Hello. I'm Michael Race, have a seat."

"Okay, Anthony, I'm here," Michael began. "First off, I don't take kindly to people lying to me. Secondly, if you lie to me once, I will not help you, do we understand each other?" he asked.

He was a serious man. I mean, he was a retired detective with the experience of knowing the streets.

"Why do you think they picked you and your codefendant to charge for this murder, Anthony?" Michael asked.

I could feel the perspiration running down my back. Why was I nervous? Could it be that I had a scent of hope in the air and didn't want to blow it?

"I don't know. Their only witness was a crack user who said she'd seen us commit the crime two blocks away," I said.

"Two blocks away? What kind of vision does she have?" Michael asked. "Do you have your DD-5's and other paperwork, Anthony? After reading your letter, I decided to take this trip up here to see you. Would you agree to a polygraph?"

I didn't hesitate as I stared at the man sitting across from me. If he wanted to give me a polygraph test to confirm my innocence, I'd do it. If he wanted to place me in front of a wall and have a thousand lights shine on me, I'd do that too. I had nothing to fear and everything to gain.

"Yes, sir, I'd comply with your test or anything else you might need of me," I said.

Michael stared at me.

I didn't blink as I returned his stare with honesty. I wasn't bashful in trying to get assistance toward my freedom and proving my innocence.

"Would Chris also agree to a polygraph?" Michael asked.

I blinked.

"You see how this works, Anthony, is that since you're both charged with the same crime, you both have to do the polygraph."

Chris was like a mule when it came to the simplest things. There was some mental blockage in his way of thinking. He thought someone was always trying to manipulate him. But even a thick-headed person like him had to see freedom looking at him and agree to the polygraph...I hope.

"Chris will agree to it as well," I said.

"Okay, then, I'm your investigator. I will start going over your trial and your minutes of the trial as well as interviewing those involved in your prosecution," Michael said. He offered me his hand. "I hope this turns out good for all of us."

I shook his hand with a firm, determined effort.

A few months later, I was sitting in my cell, reading the newspaper when the CO placed mail on my bars. I reached up and took it off without really looking at who's written me. I placed it beside me and continued reading the paper.

As the evening casually rolled in sometime later, I glanced at the letter that had been on my bed. It was the address that caught my eye. It was my old address in Albany Projects. I was perplexed. It was a name I didn't recognize. I picked it up while reading the name of the person who'd written it. Kimmy Straub. For some reason, the name struck hard in my memory. Where had I heard that name before? I couldn't place the name immediately, so I opened the letter and began to read it.

With each word I ingested, my breath became shorter, and my eyes grew wide in shock. The more I read, the more my heart pounded, the quicker my eyes blinked with each word. I continued to read the two-page letter, and when I was at the end of the letter, I slowly sat down on my bed. I stared at the ceiling as I gingerly placed the letter on top of my chest as I lay down. I felt a tear run down the right corner of my eye, and then my other eye watered as another tear rolled down my left eye. My hands trembled as the thought of what I read began to slowly sink in. I had to get to a telephone.

The next day, I was speaking to Sue, the secretary of a renowned lawyer in New York City. Sue and I had become comfortable with each other over the past three months when I asked Ron Kuby, a criminal and civil rights lawyer to take my case. I had been writing him for years in hope that he might represent me.

At first, he ignored my request, but he relented when I asked Michael Race to give him a visit. Mr. Kuby had asked Michael Race to bring some concrete evidence of my innocence to him to examine. That visit, of course, led to Ron Kuby asking his partner, Daniel M. Perez, to represent the case for their firm.

Now as I waited for Dan to get on the phone, I could feel the cold biting through my bones as I was standing in the yard outside. Dannemora was a harsh prison and made sure every inmate knew it by its astute demeanor.

"Anthony, how are you?" Dan asked over the telephone.

My mouth was dry, and my lips were cracked as I tried to find the words I was looking for. I'd been up all night reading the letter over and over. I had to slow down my thoughts to get my words right before saying them.

"Anthony?"

I still couldn't find my voice.

"Anthony?" Dan said again. "What's wrong?"

"Arlet Chestnut, Dan. I received a letter from a woman living in Albany Projects who says her boyfriend, Arlet Chestnut, wrote her a letter saying Chris and I were doing time for a crime he'd committed. This is what we've been looking for! Can we get her to testify?" I said as excitement filled my mind. "This is a woman who's saying that her boyfriend has confessed to the crime I stand accused of."

"Okay, Anthony. Calm down. Let me get the specifics. Why would this woman write you this information? Is she legit? Could this be a domestic issue where she's trying to implicate him because they are going through something emotionally? There are so many gray areas with this," Dan said.

As I listened to Dan, I felt my joy deflate like a sharp needle punctuating a balloon. Dan was right on the subject legally. There was more to the story. There had to be, I told myself. Hope had scantily brushed against my cheek and fleetingly ran away from me with a blink of an eye.

"Anthony, I'm sorry. I know you think you have something going with this one, but there are variants that we don't see at the moment, and if we're not careful, we can become entangled in legal issues we don't need to confront as this stage. Be patient."

Dan was right. The law was as finicky as a three-dollar bill. You can take a bite into it and it can be either sour or sweet. I knew this. I'd been doing paralegal for years and understood the flippancy of it.

"Anthony, let Michael Race handle the letter that was sent to you. That's his job to investigate. To soften the blow, Ron asked Sarah Wallace to give you an interview about your case."

"Sarah Wallace?" I asked.

"Yes. The news reporter on Channel 7. Sarah Wallace," Dan said.

It still hadn't dawned on me as to who he was talking about.

"Anthony," Dan began with a tone of patience. "You see her on television regularly. Just think it through. Sarah...Wallace."

"Oh, Sarah Wallace," I said as the image of her face filled my mind. "Yes, I know who you're talking about now. She wants to do an interview with me?"

"Yes, Anthony. I will set up everything. This gives your case a wider exposure and places pressure on the prosecution to rectify a painful error on their part."

"Thanks, Dan."

"No problem, Anthony. Take care of yourself, and call me if you have any questions," Dan said.

"Okay," I said.

When I hung up the telephone, I was dejected to a point, but not to a degree of total defeatism. There was nothing I could do but wait it out concerning Arlet Chestnut. I had to sit back and let the cards fall as they may, but I knew when they did fall, I would be standing tall and holding a royal flush.

That night, I began to research my files, and when I got to the Kings County District Attorney folder, I came across a document that I most recently received from the DA office that had never been disclosed in the past. It was a latent fingerprint report that stated that fingerprints were found on the cab but that they did not belong to any of the defendants accused. However, the prints remained active.

Although I'd been transferred, I still continued my job as a grievance advocate. I was doing just that as I walked into C-Block. One inmate wanted to grieve a CO who he'd felt was rude and disrespectful toward him. There'd been a heated argument in which the CO had threatened to hit the inmate with his nightstick. What took place following that was shadowy at best. The inmate reported that the CO had begun calling him racial, derogatory names, which made him begin calling the CO racial names. In the end, though, the CO came out on top, and the inmate was charged as the aggressor. As I stood in front of his cell, I was amazed at how tall he was. He had to be six feet, eight inches. While sitting on his bed, he was nearly as tall as me, and I'm five feet, six inches.

"How's it going?" I began as I opened my legal folder and took out a writing pad. "My name is Shan. Tell me what took place between you and the CO four days ago."

"Hey, bro. My name is Shawn, you can probably tell by my southern accent I'm not from New York," he said.

"CO Braw asked me to step out of line because he said my shirt wasn't tucked in my pants. I told him no matter how many times I stick it in, it's going to come out because of my height. And when I said it, I was trying to put the shirt back in my pants when he stepped closer toward me and began screaming."

"Did you start screaming back at him?" I asked. I had to intensify my hearing to get through Shawn's accent. "Were you intimidating toward him at any time?"

"No. When he stepped towards me, I gave him room by stepping back against the wall. You know how these COs are up here in these mountains. If they can get away with killing you, they'd do it," Shawn said as he nodded. "While stepping back, he began calling me 'nigger this, nigger that.' You're scum and crazy things like that, you know?"

Looking at Shawn, I could tell he wasn't lying. When he talked, he held my gaze. Usually when a person is lying, they look away to get their thoughts together to continue their lies. Prison taught me that. A person's eyes were the mirror of their essence.

"Write out what happened, and I will investigate it with a grievance," I said, as I began digging into my legal pouch that contained papers. "Don't worry about any reprimand from the officer or his friends."

"Come on, man, those white folks don't scare me," Shawn said.

I held out a paper and a pen.

Shawn looked at them as if they were something that might bite him.

"Here you go," I said, pushing them further toward him.

I watched him begin to shake his head. "Shan, I don't know how to read or write," Shawn said.

It took me a minute to adjust to what he just told me. It shocked me at this time and age that grown men didn't know how to read or write. I didn't want him to think that I was thinking ill of his misfortune, so I smiled as I took back the paper and pen.

"Shawn, it's good. I will write everything up as if you'd written it, and then read everything back to you and all you have to do is remember what was written," I said.

"You'd do that for me, man? I really appreciate you taking the time to help me out with this."

"No problem," I said. "Start from the beginning, and don't leave anything out," I said as I placed my things on the floor and sat down as I prepared myself to start writing.

My stay in Dannemora lasted a year before I was transferred to Shanwagua Prison. I once said that all prisons were the same in their makeup. And Shawagua was not different. I arrived there in January 2001. No matter what prison I was transferred to, I immediately picked up on my routine of helping others with grievances or writing my letters of freedom. I had programmed myself to ignore other things that inmates had come to rely on in prison. It wasn't my thing. I could never get into those things.

The letter that I received from Ms. Straub was on my mind so hard and I made Mr. Race and Mr. Perez aware of the fact of the latent fingerprint reports that I had obtained from the district attorney office through a FOIL request.

It was weeks later when the legal mail arrived, and it was a document from Kuby and Perez law firm. It was a motion asking the court to compel the district attorney's office to identify the owner of the latent fingerprints found inside the cab some fourteen years ago and to match them to the name of the person that Ms. Straub had indicated had informed her that he was the actual killer of the cab driver.

It was the middle of May of that year. I was lying in bed when CO Battier woke me.

"Faison, why were you in my bedroom this morning when I opened my eyes?" CO Battier asked.

I still had the sandman in my eyes when I rolled over and saw him standing in front of my cell talking.

"Your face is plastered all over television and the newspapers, Faison," Battier continued. "Get up and pack your things. The superintendent of security is here to escort you somewhere."

What was Battier talking about? I asked myself as I stared at him. I'd been up most of the night writing letters and was confused. Why was the superintendent of security there?

"Faison, you never seemed guilty to me. I've been doing this job for eighteen years, and I can tell when a person is creating a lie to go along with their story. You've always had me stumped. There were nights I would walk by and see you writing those letters, which always made me think there was more to you than the average inmate. Come on, hurry up and get your things. Don't keep the superintendent waiting."

I watched CO Battier walk away, shaking his head. I didn't know what I'd done, but whatever it was, the superintendent of security was not to be taken lightly. They were transferring me somewhere, I thought as I began throwing my legal papers and family pictures into a burlap bag. I was moving quickly while brushing my teeth and washing up in the small sink.

When the cell bars opened thirty minutes later, I cautiously stuck my head out and looked down the tier. I was expecting to see five or ten COs looking intimidating, but instead, I saw the superintendent of security standing there with three other COs. I stepped out of my cell and began walking towards them.

"Faison, my name is Superintendent Douglas of Security. Did you pack your things?" he asked.

I was nervous. I cleared my throat. "Yes, sir," I said apprehensively. I still didn't know what was going on. "Is there a problem, sir?"

"I need you to come with us," Superintendent Douglas said.

I watched him spin around on the heels of his black shiny shoes and walk away. The other two COs took a step back to give me room to follow him.

I was confused as I followed the three men. Had I finally been singled out for helping others with filing their grievances to the point that they were now going to take me to a dark hold somewhere in the prison and bury me?

We walked through the corridor in silence. We walked for ten minutes until we reached the clothing area of the prison. I was ushered into the room by one of the COs.

"Faison, enjoy your life," Superintendent Douglas said.

Enjoy my life? What did that mean? I asked myself as I watched the men walk away. My heart was racing as I glanced around, expecting something to happen.

"Faison!" A booming voice behind me shouted. It nearly made me jump out of my skin. "Get over here and put these on!"

I turned around to see an old, wrinkled, white man, who'd probably been living down in the basement for decades staring at me as he chomped down on a cigar.

"Let's move it, Faison. I don't have all day."

"Where am I going?" I asked as I walked further into the room. "People are telling me to go here and do this and that, but what's going on?"

"Put that suit on that is on the table, Faison. There are shoes and socks as well that will fit you. Come on, get moving!"

I walked to the table that was a few feet away. I'd been getting naked in front of men for years, so I had no inhibition about taking off my clothes as the grouchy CO turned his back and began writing on a clipboard. That was as much privacy as I was going to get. In fifteen minutes, I was dressed. The suit was gray and definitely out of style.

"I'm ready. Now where am I going?" I asked. What was once fear had now turned into anger. I didn't like being told what to do without letting me know why I was being told to do it. "Now what?"

The CO looked up. He stared at me. "Go through that door to the right," he said.

I glanced at the door. He wanted me to go through it without an escort? That was suspicious. Why? What was behind the door? Was there someone looking to harm me when I walked through it?

"Faison! Get going!"

I inhaled deeply. I picked up my personal belongings. I looked at the door and then glanced down at my state greens that were lying on the floor. I didn't know what was going on, but I would face it like I'd faced everything else while doing time. I walked toward the door.

As I opened the door, I was confronted with another heart-wrenching sight. Three burly-looking white men in crisp new suits were standing there staring at me. It didn't look right to me. All that was going on didn't look right to me. I was taking a step back when I was halted.

"Mr. Faison. My name is Detective Grains. The man to my right is Detective Stringer, and the man to his right is Detective Reigns from the District Attorney's office. You need to come with us."

Detectives? Was this a set-up? Had I been charged with another bogus crime? I asked myself as Detective Reigns approached me while removing a pair of handcuffs.

"Put your bag down and turn around so I can cuff you," Detective Reigns said.

I was dumbfounded as I dropped my bag and turned around. What was going on? I cringed as I felt the handcuffs snap with a deafening sound of permanency around my wrists seconds later.

Detective Stringer and Reigns took hold of each arm while Grains picked up my property. They led me out another door in silence.

I was tense with every step that I made. My increased heart rate made my breaths short. We were walking toward the front entrance of the prison. I let myself be tugged and pulled with no resistance. Minutes later, we were standing in front of the gigantic doors that either brought inmates in or let inmates go out. In my situation, I didn't know if either instance applied to me.

There was a car waiting for us as we continued to walk. We entered the car. The car drove out of the metal gate. I looked around as the car moved quickly. We were a mile out of view when the car gradually began to slow down until it stopped.

I watched as Detective Grains, who was sitting in the passenger seat, turned around and looked at me. "Uncuff him, Reigns," he said.

I was flabbergasted. Why were they taking the cuffs off me? This wasn't right, I thought, as I felt the handcuffs being unlocked.

"Mr. Faison, I'm from the District Attorney Investigation Department in New York City," Detective Grains began. "It has been brought to our attention that a man named Arlet Chestnut was picked up, interviewed, and has admitted to the crime you'd been convicted for, and we express our deepest apologies for your imprisonment and the injustice you've faced over the years."

My mouth fell open. I looked from one face to the other. How do I respond? What was I supposed to say? My tears said it all as I closed my eyes and cried and thanked the Lord for this moment.

"We are taking you to Brooklyn Supreme Court," Detective Stringer said.

He was sitting beside me. I glanced at him. I nodded, and then I leaned my head back as the reality of what was taking place sunk in. It was ten-thirty in the morning. I was going home. And for the first time in fourteen years of imprisonment, I could breathe. I could inhale air that smelled fresh and unrestricted. I looked around and then up toward the sky. It was a clear, blue sky, and it was beautiful.

As we drove to Brooklyn Supreme Court, I'd spoken to my mother and sister on the telephone. Detective Stringer had given me his cell phone, and I'd talked incessantly. It felt like an hour, but I knew it couldn't have been more than forty minutes. My mother cried, and my sister laughed. The conversation was very warm to my heart.

By the time we'd reached Brooklyn Supreme Court, we were met by a multitude of reporters waiting in front. Detective Grains decided to enter through the back of the court rather than have me face the media circus. I appreciated his kindness by nodding my head in agreement.

I was hurriedly rushed into a holding cell minutes later where I was greeted with the sight of Chris.

"Anthony, man, this is crazy, huh?" Chris said, as he paced the cell like an impatient lion waiting to hit the bars running. "I was in my cell, and I was told to get my things ready, and they brought me here. What's this all about?"

I sat down on the wooden bench. There were two paper bags on the bench. "It's about getting some justice, Chris. It's about me reaching out to thousands of people in government and other organizations to help us when all else failed. It's about freedom," I said.

Chris nodded as he stared at me. I knew he was feeling a sense of guilt for the way he'd been acting towards me when we were in Green Haven. The way he'd been creating rumors that he knew weren't true had now come back to bite him on his butt.

"Our people brought us some clothes in those bags," Chris said.

I stared at him. Sure, I could've continued berating him, but for what. I knew in his heart he felt terrible and me kicking sand in his face wouldn't change a thing. Sometimes, you have to know when to let sleeping dogs lie, I thought.

"Let's change into what they brought for us," I said, as I began removing my prison suit. "We might as well go out into the street, the way we came in."

Chris and I sat in the holding cell until two o'clock that afternoon when two COs came and got us to take us in front of Judge Kreindler. The same judge who'd sentenced us fourteen years prior. The sight before me as I walked out into the courtroom made me cringe. I was confronted with crowds of reporters, family members, and other people who probably were there simply because the crowd was there. I saw Ron Kuby standing beside the defense table. To my right, I saw the Assistant District Attorney Hawthorne. Dan mentioned him on numerous occasions. Chris and I were directed toward our lawyer.

A quiet took hold of the spectators as Judge Kreindler entered and sat down.

"ADA Hawthorne," Judge Kreindler began. "I believe we are here because there is new discovery evidence that wasn't presented at trial."

Hawthorne stood up. His suit was impeccable, I thought, as I glanced over at their table. The courtroom was packed with spectators, news reporters, and family. I saw Sarah Wallace in the crowd as well. She'd done a piece about my story a few months earlier. She waved at me when I'd entered, but I didn't want to draw attention in waving back at her. I was still amazed at what was taking place in front of me.

"Your Honor," Hawthorne began. "Uh, we have a situation here that isn't very...well, it isn't beneficial to the State of New York, but it's morally right to pursue, and I would like to bring new evidence into this sensitive case regarding Mr. Anthony Faison and Mr. Chris Light."

Judge Kreindler looked at Hawthorne. "We've walked down this path before, sir. These two men were found guilty by a jury of their peers," he said. "They were fairly given an opportunity to prove their innocence by law, and all the evidence they requested was given to them during their trial."

"Yes, Your Honor, but new evidence of these two men has come to our attention—"

"Wasn't something like this in the past presented?" Judge Kreindler asked.

"The new evidence has been corroborated by the New York City detectives who have a man in custody at this time by the name of Arlet Chestnut who has admitted to the crime Mr. Anthony Faison and Mr. Chris Light have been convicted of, Your Honor," Hawthorne said.

"And this admission of guilt has been documented by your office?" Judge Kreindler asked.

"Your Honor, if I may," Ron Kuby said, as he stood up. "We have an affidavit signed by Carolyn Van Buren, the only witness to this crime, who has recanted her story and says that she didn't see my clients at the scene of said crime. I would also like to note that Carolyn Van Buren has recanted her story on a video. With further evidence, the investigator that was hired noted also that neither Mr. Anthony Faison nor Mr. Chris Light's fingerprints were found in the cab in which they'd supposedly been in to commit this horrendous crime. Also, upon further investigation, there was no DNA of either of my clients present in the cab. Yet there was a fingerprint of Mr. Arlet Chestnut's found in the cab. This new discovery evidence is presented to the court in hopes of reinforcing these two men's innocence. Speaking to the district attorney's office, we are here today to ask that my clients be released due to the injustice that has befallen them."

I noticed as I sat in my chair that there was an eerie silence that had fallen over the courtroom. This was the same judge who'd presided over my trial and who'd convicted me. His words were like stone. How would he handle having his own case overturn? It was something that I couldn't fathom as I clutched my hands tightly. I could feel perspiration running down the middle of my back. My breathing had become shallow. Would he listen to the evidence brought before him? Would he dismiss the evidence on the grounds that it wasn't enough to overturn my conviction? Would he ignore everything and send me back to prison? Can I survive that life after coming so close to being free? I closed my eyes. I didn't close them to pray, I closed them because I was tired. I was tired of enduring the years of struggling to prove that I was innocent. I closed them because I'd hit a point of no return. I refused to be sent back to a world of darkness. I sat there and willed myself to be free.

I placed an image of my children, my mother, sister, and my father in my mind. Prison had taken so much from me. My childhood, my connection with my children as a parent, my closeness of my parents and sister, my love for a woman who'd rode bumpy roads with me, and they'd stolen my freedom. A freedom that had been ripped from my soul by lies and deceit. My soul! They'd beaten me with law. Smashed in my heart with cold-hard facts of law, and when that same law came back into play to exonerate me, they try to find an even greater form of law to deny me.

I began shaking my head as my eyes stayed closed. No, I thought. They will give me my freedom. I'd done nothing wrong! Here was evidence saying I was innocent. I felt my muscles tense with anger. I'd held my anger for years as I'd concentrated on getting my freedom, but now as I sat there listening to the law being bickered with and being tossed around lightly, my anger began to boil. I wanted to leap from my chair and scream. To let the world know that justice shouldn't be prejudicial. There was a man who'd confessed to the crime I'd been wrongfully convicted of, and they were still denying me justice. What gall do these men have that call themselves guardians of the law? They were puppeteers with no conscience.

No. I had to calm myself. I'd made it through fourteen years of keeping my head on my shoulders. I'd written over sixty-six thousand letters to get at that moment, and I'd done it through meticulous writing and patience. I will not let the world see me fall due to the shenanigans of the legal world. No, I will not let my emotions become my downfall at that moment of time. At the crucial instance when the world was watching me. I opened my eyes, and I listened.

"Mr. Hawthorne, what do you say about this new evidence?" Judge Kreindler asked. "It appears that the defense has done most of your job."

"Your Honor, after thoroughly examining the new evidence, I believe that Mr. Anthony Faison and Mr. Chris Light have both been wrongfully convicted of this crime," Mr. Hawthorne said.

"Mr. Faison and Mr. Light, life is a finicky thing. We can't read people's minds to see if they're telling the truth or not. We can only go with what we have and hope and pray that is the truth," Judge Kreindler said.

I looked into Judge Kreindler's face. The man had shattered my life by not giving me the opportunity to marry the woman I'd loved, and now he's making statements full of compassion, I thought. It was ironic.

"Mr. Faison. Mr. Light. You're free to go," Judge Kreindler said.

I was stunned as the courtroom erupted in joyous shouts. I looked around as the reality of what had just transpired fell hard on top of me. I was free. I was a free man! I told myself. Was it real? I felt Ron Kuby gently touch my left arm. I slowly rose out of my chair while leaning heavily on Ron Kuby. He kept me by his side as he guided me out of the courtroom. There was a massive throng of people in the corridor as we made our way out. There were people I'd never even seen before walking up to me and kissing and hugging me. It was surreal. I returned their hugs and kisses as I continued to be led out.

When I saw the front entrance of the Brooklyn Supreme Court, I stumbled. Within thirty feet of me was New York City in its most magnificent ambience. It was the middle of May 2001, and I was about to enter a new world that didn't have bars on the front door, nor rules or debasing searches of any private parts of my body; there would be no more curfews or lights out at eleven o'clock at night. It would be a world that I could set my own agenda. I walked out and took a deep breath. It smelled good. I was my own man now, and I'd proven that to the world.

The crowd in front of me was mindboggling. Cameras were flashing everywhere I turned. There was a podium with over fifteen microphones on it. I stepped up to the podium. The world wanted to hear a free man speak. Yet for that moment, I wanted to feel the sun on my face. I wanted to suck in the sights around me and feel the warmth of life fulfilling my body once again.

"Mr. Faison, would you like to speak?" a reporter called out to me.

Did I want to speak? That was a good question. Did anyone want to hear the words of a man who'd lived in a dungeon for fourteen years? Was silence really golden? Only if you were trying to hide something would it be golden. I, on the other hand, had seen and read a few legal documents of men in prison who were there for no other reason than being in wrong places at wrong times and having incompetent lawyers who represented them to place them in prison. I would be no different if I didn't voice my dissent for a judicial system that had wrongfully convicted me on the evidence of a drug addict who, along with another conspirator, concocted a plan to receive five hundred dollars from TIPS to purposely place me at the scene of a crime, in which I'd done nothing wrong. So yes, I did have something to say.

"I am happy that Chris and I have found our freedom today," I began, as I looked around in the audience surrounding me. "Let us not forget that the judicial system is flawed in its standing. That's evident by the fact that I am walking out of a courtroom that had convicted me and sentenced me to twenty years to life. There are men just like me in prison who have been wrongfully convicted of crimes and need to be exonerated. I thank you for this opportunity and so does my family. Chris would like to say something."

As I moved away from the podium to let Chris speak, I saw someone who made me smile. Out in the mass of bodies, I saw Critter. The man who'd kept his word and didn't forget about me over the years. We'd written each other as well as communicated with each other's family. He'd also made an effort in coming to visit me over the years. The warmest part of it all, he'd made me the godfather of his daughter. Critter was crazy as a bedbug, but had a loyal heart.

Chris's speech was short and to the point. He was never one to mince with words. As he stepped away from the podium, Ron Kuby gave a brief statement, and the next thing I knew, Chris and I were being rushed down the stairs and into the back of a car. I pulled Critter into the car with us. He was surprised, but went along anyway. We were headed to a secluded place to give Sarah Wallace an exclusive interview. Sarah deserved it. She'd done nothing but positive things for me by running my story on television, which helped in opening a doorway to my freedom.

𝔄 𝔑𝔢𝔴 𝔅𝔢𝔤𝔦𝔫𝔫𝔦𝔫𝔤

(Summer 2001-2002)

As the whirlwind of my release continued to hit the airways and television, I'd found myself staying at my sister's apartment to gather my thoughts. I'd pulled Critter in to be my agent and middleman. He could handle the bombardment of the offers of interviews, radio, and television, and I could count on him to guide me when I'd get lost. I was a star of sorts. Everyone wanted to hear from the man who'd written his way out of prison by writing over sixty-six thousand letters. Over the course of that summer, I did the Montel Show along with Michael Race. I did the Iyanla Vanzant Show. There was a radio interview at Hot 97. I did the BET Show via live connection and had a conversation with Rubin (Hurricane) Carter, another wrongfully convicted man who'd done time in New Jersey. Critter set me up with speaking engagements that gave me the opportunity to speak to people young and old about my experience.

During those speaking engagements, I wanted to convey to everyone that my strength of living through those years came from knowing I'd committed no crime. I wanted to express to those listening to me that a man caught up in the judicial system is always guilty until proven innocent. How can you beat a judicial system that was created to ensure that you get convicted?

Sure, they tell you that you'll have your chance at trial to prove your innocence, but that is a farce. If you're not given proper representation, then how can you prove that you're not guilty? I witnessed the quid pro quo of the judicial system. Lawyers are friends with district attorneys. District attorneys are good friends with judges. A wink here, a pat on the back there, and it all goes away to a point. You give me this conviction, and I'll give you the next one. Women and men are nothing more than career stepping-stones for these professional manipulators of a judicial system that sees no wrong in their actions. How can I make this statement? I'd lived through it, I'd seen it, and now I was going through the pains of finding a life for myself fourteen years later.

I'd begun to reconnect with my children. My son was now fourteen years old. My daughter Monique had conceived and made me a grandfather. I looked good to be a grandfather though. Yet all humorous thoughts aside, I was a parent again, albeit a late parent. I stood tall in my responsibilities and began to connect. Where do you enter into an adult's life as an absent parent? I had to slowly work my way into my daughter's life. Hell, she was a woman now with her own children, and I didn't want to crowd her or make her feel uncomfortable in my presence. It was a slow process, but she and I found our space and began working out the kinks in our father-daughter relationship. As for my son, Antwan, it was tense. Mind you, his mother and I had grown apart, and she'd had several more children since my incarceration. I wasn't upset with her that she'd moved on with her life. Why should I be? She'd been as loyal to me as to be expected. We were on good speaking terms. We had to be. We had a son together, and his well-being and mental state was a priority with me.

One night as I lay in my room at my sister's apartment, I was staring at the ceiling and a sense of déjà vu engulfed me. I smiled. No longer was I in a cell but in an atmosphere of freedom, but that tingling feeling touched the back of my neck. No one teaches you how to do time if you've never done it before, and no one teaches you how to integrate back into society after so many years, you have to find your niche all over again. I wasn't getting paid for my speaking engagements, and I wouldn't accept money to tell the truth anyway. Yet I knew that I had to get a job. I refused to take any handouts from anyone. I'd always been a person to get my own, and anything less than that would make me feel uncomfortable. I'd done construction work before getting arrested, but most of those jobs were now union controlled. I needed something that would help me reach out to others. I'd been helping others for so long that I'd always made myself come second, and being out was no different...to a point.

As I lay in bed, I tried to see how men like me survived in the street after being let free. I walked out of a courtroom with nothing but my personal items, my journal, and the clothes on my back. The thought of the judicial system reaching out to me and offering some assistance to get me back on my feet never crossed their arrogant minds. Unlike a war veteran when released from the service, they do get assistance to return back to the mainland. Yet men like me who had everything taken from them by a wrongful conviction received not one iota of a helping hand. Not a check. Not a monthly stipend. Nothing! When a person is processed when coming into an upstate prison, they receive clothing, shoes, socks, blanket, sheets, coat, towel, soap, washcloth, and underwear. A man or woman being released from prison receives nothing.

I began spending time at my lawyer's office in downtown Manhattan during the week as I continued to integrate myself back into society. The secretary, Sue, always made me laugh so I enjoyed dropping in. It was nearing the end of the year, and Ron Kuby along with his partner Dan Perez had filed a thirty million dollar lawsuit against the state of New York for wrongful conviction on my behalf. Dan would take the case and Ron would fly as his copilot. The thirty million dollars sounded over the top, but I was told by Dan that it was more bluster than substance. He wanted to get the attention of the attorney general to show that we were serious, and that any settlement would have to be big enough to accommodate me. Dan was shrewd and recommended that I go see a psychologist. I surmise that anyone who'd done what I'd been through needed someone to talk to. I agreed to speak to the psychologist. Now what you need to ask yourself is what can a psychologist get out of me that I haven't already received? That's the question.

Three months later, I was sitting in the waiting office of Dr. Harold K. Platz. As I sat there listening to the secretary answer calls, I looked around the office. It was painted in bright, attractive colors. Eggshell blue. white and minted green. Being that I had psychology as my minor in college while in prison, I understood the effects of the bright colors. The mind was like a sponge. It picked up and absorbed anything that the eyes came in contact with. The brain was nothing more than a large electric stimulus that functions to keep everything running swiftly. Yet it was like a CPU as it sucked in everything it saw. That is the long and short of its purpose. I could go into the deeper dynamics of its existence, but for what. You get the picture. So as I sat watching the world in front of me, I let my mind relax. My wait for Dr. Platz wasn't long.

I realized in prison that men who worked academically carried themselves differently than say a man who received a bachelor's degree. Men with PhDs exuded an arrogance of confidence in their walk. The way their shoulders stood out during simple conversation. Dr. Platz was no different. Prison taught me perception in its highest form comes from reading a person's face. I stood up and greeted him. He was a man of average height with large glasses. His hair was receding in the front, and specks of gray were in his full beard. He had to be about forty-eight years old, I thought.

"Mr. Faison. It is a pleasure to meet you. Ron Kuby asked me to assist you in your readjustment into society. Please come into my office," Dr. Platz said.

I followed him.

"Your ordeal is not uncommon, but few men or women have the opportunity to sit down with someone in a high profession as mine and release their frustration, anger, or resentment. My job is to walk you through these hang-ups of sorts," Dr. Platz said. "Have a seat."

I took the corrective chair. The one that was facing the doctor's desk. I watched him as he walked behind his desk and sat down. He reached for a pad and pen.

"Do you mind if I take notes while we talk, Anthony?"

"No, it's fine," I said.

"Let me begin by saying that I think you are an amazing person. Not too many people can write themselves out of prison. How many letters had you written before being freed?" Dr. Platz asked.

I smiled. I knew this strategy. It was basic 101 in psychology. Dr. Platz was breaking the ground to give me a comfort zone in initiating my positive feedback.

"I had written well over sixty-six thousand letters," I said.

"Remarkable. I don't know what prison is like, so enlighten me with your experience," Dr. Platz said. "But if there is anything that you're uncomfortable with talking, then please, you don't have to mention it. I want you to tell me what is going on with your life now."

Hmm. So he is giving me the opportunity to lead. I crossed my ankles as I stretched out my legs. "I've only been in the streets a few months," I began. "Yet I've been in prison for fourteen years. It's a slow adjustment." I watched the doctor nodding his head in agreement. "Prison has a way of making you appreciate everything that was taken from you. You miss the intoxicating smell of a woman's body when she steps out of a shower and sprays perfume on her body. You miss the freedom to walk down the street to go to a movie just on the spur of the moment. There is the lost feeling of having no say-so as to when you want to do something while doing time. It could be the simplest thing like staying up an extra hour to watch television or use a telephone whenever you desired it. Prison was created to strip a person of all things humane. Its sole purpose of creation is to demean, debase, castrate, and submit to all things authoritative."

"During my time inside, I had one thing going for me that kept me strong each night when it was time for me to close my eyes, Dr. Platz. I knew when I opened them the next morning, my determination would be heightened tenfold in hopes of getting my freedom. I had no guilt to ridicule my soul. I'd committed no crime to be in prison, and that knowledge compelled with the fact that I wouldn't sit in a cell and let time waste me. I refused to let my sorrow keep my head under a bucket of self-pity. The day I was sentenced was the day I began to fight, and I continue to fight as we sit here talking. I will fight for the injustice of every person that has been wrongfully convicted, and I will fight against a judicial system that is blind and deaf to the cries of men and women locked away and trying to prove their innocence. There may not be many Anthony Faisons in the world, but the one sitting in front of you is the one who cares," I said.

"Mr. Faison, I am really impressed by your sober outlook. Some men or women might take this opportunity to denounce the world for their injustice. You, on the other hand, have balanced it with a strong mental perception of what you can do to help others. That is a rare quality in a man. I see no anger in you. No resentment toward an establishment that wrongfully imprisoned you on the word of a known addict. I was expecting you to sit before me and condemn everything on the face of this earth. You're a strong man, stronger than most men I've met in my profession."

"If I hated the world, Doctor, would it change yesterday? Hate has a tendency of eating you up inside, and, Doctor, I've fought too hard to have something like that consume me. Nope, I want to live, and I want to feel healthy while I'm living," I said.

"How is your relationship with your loved ones since coming home, Anthony?"

"It's a matter of acceptance. I can look my family in the face without shame, knowing that they know that I hadn't taken another person's life, and that I'd shown the world that. A man's worth is the value he brings to the table. My worth is statuettes of virtue, Dr. Platz. I walk with my head high, and my chest out with joy. Society can never give me back the time I lost. Society can never offer me solace in which my children grew up without me. All that it can offer me is promises, and those can be forfeited at any time. No, I see it for what it is, and that is a coming of age for me. I will continue to strive for the best simply because that's all I've known since walking into prison."

"You appear to be on the right track of positivity," Dr. Platz said as he stood up. "I offer you my hand and hope that you have a stupendous life, Anthony," he said.

I took his hand as I stood up. "Thank you, Doctor." I walked out of the doctor's office, feeling happy. We'd talked for twenty minutes.

I didn't socialize with many people as freedom still grasped me with a warm feeling. I stayed in the house most of the time, but then I realized that was like staying in a cell of sorts. I paced the apartment while watching television or eating dinner. My sister would come in from work and ask me if I'd been outside. I would tell her there was nothing outside for me. She would smile and then go in the kitchen to prepare dinner. I would follow her in the kitchen and watch her. My niece would come home from school during the week and tell me about her day. She was eleven, and her cherubim, warm smile would make my day. I did this routine for two months until an old childhood friend told me to come with him to his house out in Queens. I didn't trust many people. I didn't know what their agenda was, and being that as it may, I had to always keep my guard up. I told him I'd think about it. His name was Desmond; he'd been the one who'd gotten me my construction job before getting arrested, but our relationship had deteriorated over time like all my other childhood friendships. People forget about you when they don't see you, and doing time makes you completely invisible. Prison had scarred me. I knew that. But it was those scars that kept me always expecting the worse in any given situation. Bouncing on my toes and ready to pounce if the need called for it.

It was a hot summer evening when I decided to get on the elevator and go downstairs for some orange juice. As I stepped on the elevator, I came face-to-face with a man who'd also altered my life. His name was Mickey Roper. He was the man who'd encouraged Carolyn Van Buren to tell the lie that resulted in my conviction. He'd changed over the years. He'd grown fatter, and his face looked tired and old. Sarah Wallace had done an interview with him in the hallway while standing in front of his door in which he admitted to encouraging Carolyn Van Buren to lie. We stared at each other as the elevator continued to descend.

He was the man, the mastermind who'd created my demise. I felt my nose flare. My fist clenched and unclenched as we continued to stare at each other. I'd seen that Sarah Wallace piece of filming she'd done in locating Mickey Roper. I watched on television how he'd said that he did what he did because I wouldn't vouch for him to work at my job site. At the time of that dispute, he, too, was a crack addict and was running around with Carolyn Van Buren getting high. They'd conceived their plan to split one thousand dollars for the falsely accusation of saying I'd murdered a man. Forfeiting my life was worth one thousand dollars!

"What's going on, Shan?" Mickey asked me.

I stared at him. How do you respond to a man who'd taken your life? Why wasn't I on top of this man pounding his face in with my fists? The fact that he still lived in the same neighborhood astounded me.

"Man, I want to say that I'm sorry for what we did to you," Mickey said. He took three steps toward me and offered his hand. "I was going through some hard times back then, and I wasn't thinking straight."

I unconsciously cringed away. I had to catch myself though. This was that jump over the moon moment. Were all my words of positivity going to go to the wayside if I wrapped my hands around his throat and squeezed? Was I going to be a bigger man and forgive this person who wronged me so deeply? Was it that easy? No! This man had shattered my life. He had taken away the parent that was in me so I could raise my children. Forgiveness wouldn't be that easy.

"If the situation was reversed, I wouldn't want to shake my hand either," Mickey began. "I was dumb back in those days, man. I know you've been through a lot and it was my fault. I'm just asking for your forgiveness. My life is different now. It's better. I really am sorry."

His hand was still out there. Hovering in the air...waiting.

To my surprise, I took it.

As we stood there shaking hands, I felt my whole body become lighter. My head seemed to swoon with lightness. My breathing became warm as it exhaled through my nose. We locked eyes and nodded.

"Thank you," Mickey said as the elevator doors opened.

I watched him walk away as I stepped out of the elevator. All the resentment that I'd had for him moments ago had dissipated with a shake of a hand and my forgiving him. I couldn't understand it, but I had no animosity toward the man. It was like he was walking out of my life, and I was hoping he found peace.

I walked out of the building with a spring in my step. I had forgiven a man who changed my life, and I didn't feel angry. Instead, I felt content as the fading sun touched my face. Prison had scarred me and changed me all at once. I began walking across the street when a car nearly hit me. I still hadn't gotten used to crossing the street. In prison, there weren't any streets to cross. I was about to apologize as the car drove by me until I saw the face of the driver. It was my father.

"Son, get in the car."

I crossed over and got in on the passenger side. My father slowly drove away.

"I know I haven't gotten in touch with you until now, Anthony, but you know me. I like to keep things quiet. Anyway, the way your face was plastered all over the news and those other shows, I thought you'd be too busy for me."

I glanced at my father. The years away had brought him new wrinkles on his face. His hands looked a little curled. Arthritis had begun to set in, I thought. I turned and looked straight. My father was the kind of man who kept to himself. He was never really emotional when it came to something that was close to his heart. If he felt a sense of emotion, he usually smiled rather than say what he was feeling.

"Pop, I knew I'd see you sooner than later," I said. "Thanks for sending money over the years."

I saw him smile. "You make me proud, Anthony. In my heart, I knew you couldn't have done what they'd accused you of doing. You are my son, and I've taught you better than that. Every day you were in prison, I thought about you and hoped that you'll make it to prove to the world that they were wrong. You're my hero, boy."

"You missed me, huh?" I said and laughed. "It's good to see you, Pop. Have you spoken to Mom?"

"When you first came home, we talked. You know your mother, she has her point of view and I have mine, but I don't love her any less. I told my female friend that you were my son, and she told me that you were a strong man. I put my chest out when she said that, Anthony. My seed had walked out of prison with pride."

"You mean you told your girlfriend," I said as I glanced at my father. I saw his smile widen. "You never like calling them girlfriend, do you, Pop?"

"Girlfriends and wives sound so permanent, son. Open the glove compartment and take out that envelope for me."

I opened the glove compartment and took out the envelope. It felt heavy.

"What are you doing about a job, Anthony?"

"My lawyer is trying to get me a job working with people who have AIDS," I said as I offered the envelope to my father. "It will give me an income. Right now, I have Mom and Evelyn helping me out with money."

"No, son. Open the envelope for me."

I opened it. I reached inside and pulled out a handful of money. I looked at my father.

"Relax, boy. Since you've been away, I'd opened a savings account for you and put fifty dollars in it each time I got paid. I think I did it to give you a small comfort zone when the day you did get out. I just didn't want you to hit these streets struggling for a dollar."

I was stunned.

"It's not much, but a little is better than nothing. It's seven thousand dollars. Put it up and keep quiet, Anthony. Come on, I'll treat you to dinner."

My father always could make me smile. He was a man who did what he did and never wanted anything back in return. He was a stoic man who walked alone at times, but loved his children without saying a word. I loved the man.

A few hours later, I was sitting in the car with Desmond. He was driving me to have dinner with his wife and his sister-in-law. It was good to be out and away from the cameras and interviews. I was looking forward to having something more connective.

We arrived at the restaurant that was in Queens within thirty minutes. I'd dressed the part. Dress pants, shoes, a nice shirt, and a leather coat. I think I looked good. We entered the restaurant. I didn't know what Desmond's wife or sister-in-law looked like, so I just followed him.

He led me to a table in the far corner where two attractive women were sitting. We sat down, and Desmond introduced me to them.

"Anthony, the lady to the right is my wife, Tanya, and the little one to her left is her sister, Valeria," Desmond said.

"You look...nice, Valeria," I said.

"So you're the man who has written himself out of prison. A man who controlled his future with a pen and paper. That's a rare feat," Valeria said as she smiled. "What else can you do? Can you predict the lottery numbers for me, so I can find me a bigger place to live?"

I was impressed by her directness. She was five feet, six inches. Her light skin and light brown eyes were mesmerizing. I'd known beautiful women in my life, but her beauty coupled with her satire wit gave her an approachable aura. I'd met a few women since being released, and none of them appeared to possess the fire Valeria had. And the fact that she had a breathtaking smile only intensified my curiosity.

"What do you do? Have you found a job yet? I'm sorry if I sound forward. It's just that I'm the kind of person who likes to get to the point before the point becomes pointless," Valeria said.

"I'm still adjusting to the streets. As for a job, I have one in the works," I said.

"Is there anything in particular you're looking for, Anthony? I mean, I don't want to be nosey, but they didn't give you anything to help you settle back into society?" Valeria asked. "No money? An EBT card, nothing? What about food stamps? I know what you're going through. I have a cousin who was released from prison after doing five years, and the only thing he received from the state were two beepers, ninety-two dollars, a Kango hat, one gold-plated ring, and a pair of Cazel glasses. That's what he had when he got busted, and that's what they had waiting for him when he came home."

I stared at her. No, everyone at the table stared at her. She was funny without trying to be funny. I laughed. We all began laughing at her. She was cool, I thought, as I stared at her. Cool and bright.

"I like your humor," I said as I reached for the glass of water on the table. She was easy to talk to.

"All right, seriously, I got dinner tonight," Valeria said. "Tonight, we celebrate the coming home of Anthony Faison!"

I was going to protest her generosity, but thought better of it. I nodded my head in appreciation as our eyes held each other for a moment. I smiled. She was classy. I would enjoy dinner and getting to know the woman whose lightness towards life was filled with laughter.

"I think I can handle dinner," I said. "But since I'm impressed by your laid-back demeanor, I'll let you treat me tonight. Next time, though, it's on me. What kind of work do you do?"

"Oh, so there's going to be a 'next time' between us? No one informed me." She smiled. "I work at a law firm in Manhattan. I'm a paralegal," Valeria said.

We clicked at that answer.

Four months later, I was sitting behind a desk. In front of me were the files of client's everyday progress reports regarding their continued health, psychological, and social stimuli. Ron Kuby did get me the job working with AIDS clients as he'd promised. As I became more knowledgeable with those with AIDS, I became a firebrand for them to receive their rights as individuals who have a sickness and shouldn't be denied their civil rights when requesting housing, medical, or any other benefit. Maybe it was my nature to take up for the downtrodden because I fought for them as if they were my immediate family.

I didn't know much about AIDS until I began working with the organization called Housing Works. To me, I thought people with AIDS were outcasts looking to take advantage of the benefits that were offered to them to stay home and out of society's eyes, but I was wrong as I began to know each of my clients as individuals, not as sick people waiting to die one day. When a person is uninformed of a subject, they automatically think horrible things. I would come to realize that as I began to go to court for some of my clients who were either being discriminated against due to their sickness in regards to housing, employment, or health issues. I felt like I was doing what I did best. Taking up the cause and putting all my heart into it. That was me, always advocating.

I researched AIDS during my first two months at Housing Works. I wanted to know everything about the disease. I felt like I was back in prison doing legal research at times as I read the history of AIDS. I'd always been the kind of person who didn't like to be half informed on anything. When I advocated for my clients, I wanted to let them know that I wasn't there just to get a check, but to ensure they were treated accordingly. I wanted to be more than a counselor to them.

My first client was Gloria Ruiz. She was twenty-four years old, and had been in Housing Works for a year. She lived in

Brownsville, Brooklyn, with her mother. She had no other siblings, and her father had been out of her life since she was ten years old. She was a beautiful, young lady who was very bright. She'd contracted HIV when she was eighteen years old from an older man in his thirties who'd known he was HIV positive and seduced her with words of sweetness and alcohol. He'd courted her for months to a point in which he'd begun stalking Gloria until she'd given in to his lustful ways. It had been a one-time sexual encounter with no protection, and it was that one time that brought her world to a halt when she'd been told of her condition.

She needed counseling to accept her situation, and during the course of that time, she'd tried to commit suicide three times before she was twenty years old. Yet as acceptance of her situation became clear and she grew older, she returned to school and concentrated on getting a degree in social work.

It was three days before Christmas, Gloria and I were sitting in Housing Court. She'd been subpoenaed to appear because of a rent dispute with her landlord. We had been told by the clerk that we would be seen next.

"I have a final paper to finish," Gloria whispered to me. "Do you think they will really call us soon?" she asked.

I looked at her. She smiled. "How are you coming along with your medication?" I asked. "And yes, we will be called in time for you to get home and finish your paper for school."

"Yes, I take my meds," Gloria answered. "Can I ask you something, Anthony?"

"Of course," I said as concern gripped me. I hope she wasn't going to tell me she wanted to leave school. She was making wonderful grades.

"I met this guy in school a few months ago, and we get along perfectly. Lately though, he's been wanting to take our relationship to the next level, and I've been putting it off with one excuse after another. I think he's getting impatient with me," Gloria said as she sheepishly explained her situation to me.

"What's the next level?" I asked as confusion filled my face.

Gloria smiled. "He wants to have sex with me, Anthony," she said.

I looked at her. "Okay," I said slowly. "So you told him you're HIV positive, right? And he understands your situation."

She pouted and began shaking her head. "I didn't tell him I'm HIV positive," she said.

I turned toward her. "If you're going to have sex with him, you have to tell him your situation. It is your responsibility to give him the option, Gloria," I said as sternly as possible without sounding upset.

"Why? If we're using a condom and I'm careful, then there's no need to tell him about my condition. It's like I'm sabotaging our relationship before it even begins, and that's not fair, Anthony."

"Fairness has nothing to do with this, Gloria. You're in the driver's seat, and being that you are, you have to make decisions that reflect your responsibility. While during your course of having sex with him, the condom breaks. What now?"

"It wouldn't break. I'd make—"

"You can't make sure it wouldn't break, Gloria," I said, cutting her off. "There is no guarantee that it wouldn't, only possibilities. In his mind, with the condom broken, he's thinking the worse that can happen is that you get pregnant, but you, on the other hand, know that the breaking of the condom might've altered his life completely. How does he feel when you tell him to go get tested? What is going through his mind? Will he hate you? When he asks why didn't you tell him before agreeing to have sex with him, what will you say? Remember how you contracted the disease and how you felt when the person knew they had it? You felt betrayal, and so will he if he isn't given a choice."

She turned towards me. She was crying. "You're right, Anthony. If the person who'd infected me had given me a choice, I wouldn't be in the situation I am now. I will tell him before having sex with him, and if he does agree, then it's good, if not, then at least I'd given him a choice. Thank you," she said as she reached over and hugged me.

"Choices are a good thing," I whispered in her ear. "Staying strong no matter what your situation is in life is what makes you special."

"Gloria Ruiz verses Harper Management," shouted the clerk.

Gloria and I broke our embrace and stood up. It was time to go fight for the little man, woman, once again. I enjoyed the fight, I said to myself.

Catching the Fox

(2003-2005)

My life would come full circle in the fall of 2003. My lawsuit against the State of New York had begun. Chris and I along with Critter and Beatty were standing in the corridor where my case was being heard in one of the buildings in downtown Manhattan. We were putting our brains together as to why the State of New York would oppose awarding Chris and me monies intensified with each passing day of the trial.

By acknowledging that I'd been wrongfully imprisoned for fourteen years, the State admits this with my release and the confession of Arlet Chestnut only adds to their erroneous behavior, but those things meant nothing if it means giving me any money to compensate for my lost years. No matter how many times I'd fight the judicial system, it never wanted to admit guilt in the simplest form. There were days as I went to work and back and forth to court that I felt like telling my lawyer, Dan Perez that I'd had enough. I wanted to get out of New York and build a life without the lingering smell of betrayal attached to my moral fiber. I'd been the one wronged, and still, I had to prove to the world in hopes of receiving a livelihood lost by their lack of investigative skills, resulting in me losing so many years in prison.

I had become dejected by the actions of the State of New York in their pursuit to deny me a small semblance of respect. It's like they kick sand in my face for seeking to show the world that'd I'd been imprisoned for the act of someone else, and then when I asked to be treated fairly, the system tells me that if I hadn't been in the wrong place at the wrong time, I wouldn't have been imprisoned, so why should they pay me any money.

To keep my sanity, I threw myself into my work at Housing Works while dating Valeria exclusively. She was a woman who made me laugh. She was three years younger than me, but her mentality spoke volumes of maturity. She could relate to me without me explaining myself all the time. I always made an effort to have her along at my family events. She was a sharp knife with an even sharper outlook in life.

Valeria and I had moved in together, following months of dating. We'd found a two-bedroom apartment in East New York, Brooklyn. It wasn't a grand place but is was ours to call home. I would come to find out later that Valeria had a daughter who was in the custody of her ex-husband. I loved the woman, so it didn't make any difference to me if she had a child or not. Most women had children from previous relationships or marriages in today's society, but I'd never met her. I knew her name was Crystal and she was eight years old.

One night after having a long day at work, Valeria walked into the bedroom wearing a beautiful, short, black teddy. She'd had her hair done as well as her nails. She was looking strikingly beautiful. I watched her prance around the room gathering things to iron and never once did she look in my direction. If she was wearing the teddy to go to bed in, I thought, then intimacy between us would be mind blowing tonight. I sat up on my elbows to stare at her. She ignored me as she continued walking in and out of the room. The next time she entered the room, I stopped her with a commanding playful voice.

"Valeria, I have to say, you're looking more than beautiful tonight."

Valeria put the clothing she was carrying on top of the dresser and turned around to face me. She smiled as she walked to the doorway and stood there. The light from the living room silhouetted her frame, which made me smile.

"Do you like my new piece?" Valeria asked.

"I love it. It catches all of your...attributes," I said and laughed. "You look beautiful."

"Well, thank you. I bought it specifically for you."

"Nice," I commented as my eyes took in every portion of her beautiful body. "What's the occasion? Did you get a raise or a promotion?"

"Hmm. How can I answer that," Valeria began. "As for the raise, that will kick in about four or five months from now, and the promotion should follow three months later if my calculations are right," she said.

"Why are they delaying your raise?"

I watched her walk towards me. She could be seductive when she wanted. She sat on the edge of the mattress. "Well, babies take a minute to get it together, Anthony."

"What does a baby have to do with your raise?" I asked. "Do you need me to talk to someone at your job?"

She stared at me.

"What?" I asked.

Her stare grew more penetrating.

"Okay, men act like babies sometimes, that's who we are when we don't get our way," I said and shrugged.

She crossed her arms over her chest and continued to stare.

Then the light went on in my head.

"You're pregnant?" I asked as I sat up in bed.

"I'm nine weeks," Valeria said as she stood up and walked away. When she was near the doorway, she spun back around. "So this outfit is for your viewing because in a few months, the hair, nails, and other accessories will not be looking as good when the stomach starts sticking out."

I got out of bed and walked over to her. I took her in my arms and hugged her very strongly.

"What do you think?" Valeria asked as she looked up into my face. "You're not upset with me, are you?"

I bent down and kissed her gingerly on her lips. "Well, I think we're going to need a bigger place."

Valeria laughed.

My lawsuit continued to be contested by the state as the weeks went by. When I told my family that Valeria was pregnant, everyone was happy for us. I continued to bond with my son and daughter. Trying to guide them without being too pushy. When I told Critter that I would appreciate it if he were the godfather to my son, he didn't even blink at the responsibility and agreed to it immediately. I had become more outgoing as time went by. I started to go to clubs and feel that sensation I used to feel as a young man. It was a wonderful feeling to feel the music on my skin and watch people dance. I walked around listening to the music. I'd ordered tonic water as I stood by the bar. I didn't come to pick up women. I'd come out to enjoy myself without the scrutiny of others asking me questions concerning my life since being released.

As I watched the women and men dance along with the music, I was standing in a corner as I watched a woman approach me. She was smiling and holding a drink. I looked past her. I didn't want to give her the impression that I was staring at her. I was shocked when she stopped in front of me. She was smiling when she asked me if I wanted to dance. I laughed. She couldn't be older than twenty-five years old. I was about to decline her offer when she took my hand and led me on the dance floor.

Man, I hadn't been on the dance floor in years. I stood there watching her as she swayed with the sound of a pulsing drum beat and a penetrating bass sound reverberating off the walls. It was beautiful to feel the music coming alive on my skin. I tried to stealthily look around at how the men were dancing to get into the groove of things without looking awkward. Slowly, I began to shake a hip and then moved my shoulders as the music took hold of me. Hell, minutes later, I was dancing as good as the next person. And damn it, I hadn't lost my moment as I matched the young lady dancing with me rhythm for rhythm. I danced until the sun came up, and I had a good time. It's true when they say once you learn how to ride a bike, you never forget how to pump the pedals.

Two months later, after constant bickering and humiliation, the State of New York agreed to a settlement of one million and seven hundred thousand dollars for my years of incarceration. I, on the other hand, thought there was no amount of money that could compensate for my lost years, but my attorney, Daniel M. Perez, informed me that it was the best thing to do. He said I had to let it go or else my holding on would tear me apart. I agreed with his outlook and accepted the settlement.

I never had any real friends while doing my bid, except for Critter, Beatty, Born, and a few others. Yet these men's friendships had eventually turned into a brotherhood over the years so I don't even call that a friendship anymore. The fact that the newspaper and news media had told the world about my settlement, I now became a magnet for every cousin, aunt, uncle, great-aunt, great-uncle, and any other sibling who thought they were related to me to suddenly pop out of nowhere with cries of being impoverished. I wonder how many people would be in my life when the time came when I had no more money. I gave money to those in need, but when does the need end?

By the end of 2003, I'd invested some of my money into my first house. Not an apartment but a house with a backyard that was big enough to let my newborn child run free. I wanted him to have an opportunity to breathe freely. It was a five-room family house in Rosedale, Queens, New York. The moment I received the keys to my house, I felt a sense of pride tickle through my body. I had something that was mine. A place called home where my kids could grow up and feel proud.

I had fought for my freedom. I had put my nose to the ground to the point of going insane as the years passed me by while at the same time trying to prove to the world that I, Anthony Faison, was innocent, and I'd done that. Now as I walked through my new empty house by myself, jiggling the keys, I felt euphoria. No one had ever given me anything. I'd always had the mental capacity to seek out my own wants and desires. Now sitting on the stairs of my empty house, I smiled. I felt a sense of security. My son was one year old, and I'd hoped to give him a direction in life that would lead him away from the life on the streets. I didn't want him to ever go to prison. I would forfeit my own life to prevent him from ever enduring the suffering I had. As a father, we try to maneuver our children away from the negative places we've been by encouraging them with experiences of our lives. If that meant frightening them with the real horror stories that had taken place in our lives, then it is the responsibility of that parent to make it penetrate with shocking, painful, and meaningful realism. Don't hold back for fear of alienating the child; it is that feeling you want to put the fear of God in them with your experience. I would put that fear in my child to keep him from going to prison.

Valeria was the kind of woman that didn't pester me. She would sit back and wait her turn in life. It was the summer of 2006 when I asked her to marry me. Talk about breathtaking moments. Before the words had completely exited my mouth, her arms were wrapped around my neck, and she was kissing me continuously. I could've played the man who didn't believe in marriages, but Valeria was a woman who didn't ask for much. She took care of the house, the children, and me. And she demanded nothing from me. That kind of a woman is a rarity, and I didn't want to lose her for lack of not showing how much I cared about her. Not once did she ask me to marry her. She didn't use any ruses to snare me in anyway. I could talk to her about my years in prison, and she would listen while we lay in bed and she gently stroked my chest for comfort. A woman like her was a glistening pearl that shined with brilliance even in the dark. A woman like that—from a man's perspective—you kept close to your heart. She was worth marrying. I loved her more than I loved any other woman.

Remember when I mentioned people coming out of the woodwork when the state gave me my settlement money? Well, I have an uncle, my father's brother. His name is Jasper Houden, and he and my father were half brothers. Same mother, different fathers. His nickname was Sandman. When I was a child—six or seven years old—he would drive up from South Carolina every other summer to visit, and every time that he did, he always let me travel with him no matter where he went. I can say he was my favorite uncle. My father used to say that his brother was a dreamer. There wasn't any quick buck scenario he wouldn't try if it could make him some money. My uncle was called Sandman because of his quick speaking skills. If he asked you for a dollar, by the time he finished telling you why he needed the money, you realized that you'd given him one hundred dollars.

He'd once told me that he'd sold the Queensboro Bridge in New York City to three white men in El Segundo, California, when he was seventeen years old for five thousand dollars. He said that the first two had signed the contract, and he was waiting for the last one to sign when the man's wife came out and exposed his trickery. He said that was the only time he'd nearly been shot, but that didn't keep him from continuing his shenanigans. To him, every person could be manipulated if they thought they were getting something better than what you were actually selling it for. To him, it wasn't about deception, it was about who could outthink who first to make the steal quickly. It was greed trying to outsmart another person's greed.

Now as he sat across from me in my house in the kitchen, I saw that age hadn't been kind to him. He was wearing glasses now, and what used to be a conscientious effort to wear the latest in fashionable clothing was now clothing that he'd just thrown on. It didn't make me think of him any differently. He was still my favorite uncle.

"Anthony, boy, you're looking good," Uncle Sandman said. "Damn, I like this house. Must have cost you a penny or two, huh?"

I smiled as I stared at my uncle. A hustler to the end, I thought. His question was to find out how much I spent on the house to see where my money numbers were.

"Boy, you know I'm proud of you. I knew you didn't murder anyone. Your father and I taught you better than that. How many rooms are in this house?" Uncle Sandman asked as he glanced around.

"I'm glad you thought well of me, Sandman, what brings you to New York?" I asked.

"I came up to see the family."

I arched an eyebrow to inform him that he had to come better than that.

"Oh, and I came to see you married off, boy," Uncle Sandman said.

I cleared my throat as I stared at him. Another indication that he wasn't fooling me.

"All right. All right! I came to make you a proposition that can be to your benefit without much of a downside."

There was nothing but love in my heart for my uncle as I listened to him try to convince me to invest in one of his ideas. I had to give it to him, though, he'd always been a man who went after what he thought was his dream of success, and those dreams had been many as a kid watching him pitch his schemes to my father and mother while growing up.

"You sure you want to marry this girl? I was a young man too, at one time, and these young girls tell you one thing while at the same time slapping you in the face about something else. Does her family have money? Are there any skeletons in her closet that you don't know about, and once you're married to her, then you have all these uncles and aunts coming out acting like they know you with their hands out looking for favors?" Uncle Sandman said.

Mind you, he spoke so fast that the entire paragraph seemed like it was one sentence.

"Let's hear your pitch, Uncle," I said.

"Aw, boy. It's not a pitch, it's a dream that we can turn into a reality. You ever hear of balloons with flavor?"

I was stumped. I stared at him. *Do you eat the balloons or blow them up*, I asked myself. "No, I've never heard of that. What do you do with them?"

"Well, son, you can blow them up and they leave a flavor in your mouth. See, kids blow them up while wanting to have that taste in their mouths as well. It's a catch 22 situation. You're selling the balloons with a pitch of flavor," Uncle Sandman said, as he grinned at me displaying his two front teeth, which were missing.

"So you want me to invest in your business of flavored balloons?" I asked as I leaned forward in my chair.

"Son, this isn't an investment. It's a lifetime decision to get a business off the ground before someone else thinks of it," Uncle Sandman said.

"How much money do you need to get this business off the ground?" I asked. A smile filled my face.

He looked at me. Weighing his options, I guess. He returned my smile.

"I think twenty-five or thirty thousand ought to do it, Anthony. With that kind of capital, we can hit the ground running," Uncle Sandman said.

I laughed. "You know five thousand will get us off in the right direction as well, Uncle," I said, as I watched his smile fade. "It's a small business plan and will do well with a little bit of money or lot of money. It's something new. What do you think? If not, you could always go to a bank and apply for a business loan."

"Bank? Business loan? No, no. Five thousand should get us off on the right foot. We won't be running, but at least, we'll be walking. It might be some slow steps, but we would be on our way," Uncle Sandman said.

"Walking has us in the lane, Uncle. I will write you a check, and—"

"Whoa, son. I could do better if you gave me cash. You know checks and I don't get along properly, nephew," he said.

"Okay. I will give you the cash. I will give you the money in two days after my wedding," I said.

Minutes later, I was walking my uncle to the door. I watched as he entered his twenty-two-year-old car and drove away. I stood there watching him. That car was sputtering dark smoke from the exhaust. My uncle was a special man. Not once did he deny me a money order whenever I asked him to send me money over the years while I was in prison to help me buy stamps to put on my envelopes. If I'd written him and told him I needed money for anything, he would send it. I'd never written him and asked him to come to see me, but if I did, I knew he would. He was an uncle who was a good man and a limited realist...to a point, I thought.

My son, Romello, was nearly two years old when I decided to marry his mother, Valeria. The concept of men with children not having the father's last name is common in America. I didn't want that for my son. When he was born, I was there in the birthing room. I watched the afterbirth being removed from him as he entered into this world. Better yet, I saw the pain his mother went through in the conception of my son. As a man, I want to explain to my son as my father had done to me. Men are always considered the breadwinners in the home. The leaders of the pact. Yet men are limited to their purpose in life. Sure, we begin our lives as trying to do the right thing. We want to make impressions that lead our children to meaningful lives, but there is no control in what occurs without your input. The example is correct in my own life with my wrongful conviction. A person can't see the future, but you can mold the present for the future if you can understand the past.

My wedding five months later was a trying one. I'd never done anything like preparing for a marriage before. When I was with Sherry, I had imagined that she and I would walk down the aisle in a little prison church, but my wedding to Valeria was a huge one. We'd decided to get married on Long Island, New York, and the ceremonial hall we'd rented was a big one. We had over one hundred guests arriving. There would be doves released at the conclusion of our vows. There were several bridesmaids and groomsmen. My best man at my wedding was Critter. My goddaughter, his daughter, was also in the wedding along with my grandchildren and Beatty. Beatty decided that I needed a haircut before the wedding, so I told him to give me a haircut. It was a breathtaking sight. I'd even invited Chris. He and I hadn't had a strong, friendly conversation since our release, but I didn't want to reject him by not inviting him to my wedding. That wasn't me.

Valeria was beautiful at our wedding. She glowed. Her wedding dress was something out of a fairy tale. It was cream color and fit her magnificently. I watched her being escorted down the aisle and was glad I was marrying her. I loved her and knew that she loved me. When she stood in front of me, I saw that she'd been crying. I took her hand and squeezed it affectionately. I was getting married. To the right of me stood Critter my best man and my best friend. He handed me the wedding band when the preacher finished the words of marriage. The thing about Critter is that he never discouraged me about marrying Valeria. To him, it was simple. If I was happy, then he was happy. That's a friend.

What most people didn't know was that although I'd been given a large amount of money for my settlement, I didn't put it all under my touch. Most of the money I placed in a fund to grow interest over ten years. People thought I was rich and I wasn't. With that kind of money, I would waste it on things that had no real value. But I did buy me a cell phone store in Queens, New York, in 2005. It was a business that I strived to make work. I went to work early each morning to open my store and stayed late each night. It was a profitable business, and although my business sense was limited, I surrounded myself with people who knew how to run a business.

I had to come to rely on my knowledge of business from my years in prison. If you didn't know how to do something, you paid other people to do it, and while they're doing it, you learn that skill. I became a good businessman in selling cell phones. I have always been a people person and would fill them with warmth when they entered. I didn't try to push on them any phone that didn't interest them, but I gave them comparisons in which they saw the difference between my store and the store three blocks away. People want to feel needed when they walk into any establishment. Sure, they were coming in to buy something, but they wanted you to appreciate their presence, and I mastered that concept. My business was booming, and I was happy. I was a businessman with a family. I was providing for my family, and I was happy. I'd come out from underneath a rock and set my mark on the world.

Yet reality is a brutal thing. As time passed and I concentrated on my business, I became obsessed with making sure it didn't go under due to the economic situation at the time. There were stores folding everywhere. I found myself coming home later and later each night as I stayed in the store to do the books, rearrange lights, make deals with other wholesalers, or do my inventory. Soon though, my need for success would eventually come crashing down around me, particularly in my home.

Valeria had become demanding with my presence in the house. Every night I came home, she would question me as to why I was spending so much time in the store. What answer could I say but the truth? I was running a business, and for me to succeed in that business, I had to be on top of my game. She was a woman and wanted me to spend more time at home. She wanted me to be home at a certain time for dinner and to put the children to bed together during a certain time. The thought of that visionary concept was beautiful, but making it become something of substance was difficult. I was trying to make my children's and grandchildren's lives better. I wanted to turn one cell phone store into multiple stores for them to have in the future, and to do that, I had to make sacrifices. Valeria would hear none of that. What I married as a beautiful, caring woman six months prior was turning into a jealous, unpredictable, and vindictive woman. In the short time of our marriage and living together, I watched her change into a person I didn't know.

I had come to realize that being released from prison would be a thing of bliss, but as each day passed and I saw the true nature of people enter into my life, I accepted that whether it is in prison or in the free world, people are who they are no matter what your situation might be. There will always be a fight in any arena you might encounter. I was free on the outside world, but I was now fighting people who were the people I loved. People who were either talking behind my back or plotting to do something to me. You might think I was becoming paranoid, but I wasn't. I'd become aware of the whispers that were being said about me becoming obsessed with my store and forgetting everything else. Their misconception of me was being misdirected by people who probably didn't know me or who may think they knew me but didn't. Through sheer purpose and will, I made my life different, and now, I was hearing painful things about me that were not true, and that frustrated me. There were some days I would go to bed with a splitting headache and wake up with an even more painful one.

Valeria had begun to hang out at her brother's house in St. Albans, Queens. I would come home from the store, and the house would be empty. For three weeks, this occurred until I finally asked Valeria why wasn't she coming home, and she'd informed me that if I wasn't home why should she keep coming home. From that moment on, we slowly began to have a fallout. Happiness in my life had begun to fade.

As Valeria and I continued to have our differences, our marriage had reached a degree of no return one night as I'd made an effort to get home early to have dinner with her and the children, but I would be shocked at what I saw when I entered my house.

When I walked through the front door an hour later, I saw suitcases sitting by the stairs. I heard sounds coming from the bedroom. As I walked into the bedroom, I saw Valeria's brother and his girlfriend packing up her belongings.

With the passing of weeks, Valeria and I agreed that I could have my son on the weekends. I gave her money each month to care for my son. No matter how many times I tried to convince her to return home, she wouldn't budge. She felt that I'd lost interest in her simply because I tried to ensure that my business wouldn't fold. I would realize during some of our conversations that she needed constant attention in her life, and I'd unconsciously neglected that by working so arduously. How do you confront something like that? You don't. I can't make a person see the benefits of joy. A person has to have that within to appreciate it when they see it. Valeria only saw what she wanted to see and nothing more. I accepted that fate and would come home from work to an empty house.

On night in the spring of 2007, as I sat in the living room of my empty house, I decided that New York City had taken all that I was allowing it to take from me. I'd decided that the Big Apple had become too big for me, and rather than slice it up, I decided that moving out of it was my next best choice. But where would I move? I wanted to move somewhere in which no one knew my history. It had to be a place that didn't have its ear to the ground all the time. Yet leaving New York would be painful to me. I loved the air, the people, the nightlife, and its brilliance. In the course of moving, I'd also wouldn't be in the immediate proximity of my son if he needed me to be there. No matter how old I'd become, my need to protect my family was tremendous and I was always conscientious of that fact. So how far would I move? And then, there was my business. I would have to sell it when I did move. I struggled to keep it above water, and now I was about to see it sink by selling it. Decisions are those things we want to run from, but being a man, you can't run from the things that are yours. You have to stand tall and face it down. No doubt about it. I would stand tall like I've done for most of my life. It was the balance of an equation, and I was the numerator and denominator.

By the middle of June of that year, I'd sold my business. I knew I could've received more from the buyer if I'd pressed her, but we'd come to a mutual price. I gave Valeria forty thousand dollars from the sale of my business. I gave it to her although we weren't divorced and was only separated. I didn't want to be deceptive with her regarding anything in which my son was indirectly involved in. A good man, as I understand it, is a man who can reach within his soul and know that the things he does are out of the kindness of his heart and not viciousness or contempt. When you give someone something, you don't ask for anything in return. Valeria was my wife and the mother of my son. I couldn't do anything to her that might be detrimental to my son, and I wouldn't do anything to her that might be considered unkind. She was a good woman, and we'd simply fell out.

I was driving home to my empty house one late evening after coming from my lawyer's office when I had a small accident. The car in front of me had abruptly stopped short, which in turn made me hit the back bumper. As I exited my car, I was furious. Why would a person stop short the way the driver did, I thought as I walked toward the driver side of the person's car. I was about to go at it with the driver when a pair of long legs appeared from the driver's side. I stopped to gather my thoughts and then realized that no matter how pretty the legs looked, the woman still created the accident. That reality flew out of my head when I saw her face.

Standing in front of me was a woman that was knock-dead gorgeous. Her full lips combined with her warm smile, and her perfectly clear, light skin made me take a step back as if a powerful wind had suddenly appeared and pushed me. She apologized for making the accident. Her apology was so sincere that I shrugged off the incident as if it were a minor one, but the reality of that was that the front grill of my Mercedes-Benz was severely damaged. As she continued to apologize and informed me that she'd pay for the damage, I stared at her with unblinking eyes. My first thought was how could she pay for the damage that looked like it was over three thousand dollars. What kind of job did she have to put out that kind of money, considering she was driving a six-year-old Camry. I told her that we'll work things out without relying on the insurance companies. She eagerly accepted my suggestion, and we exchanged our information as well as our telephone numbers. By the time we'd finished, I realized I might be a little smitten. I watched her as she drove away. When I turned the key in the ignition, the car didn't turn over. I tried it again and still nothing. I shook my head as I reached for my phone to call for road service.

In October of 2007, I'd sold my house and had decided that I 'd move to Atlanta, Georgia. Why Georgia? It was a faraway place from New York City and from those who always wanted to suck me dry for money. It was different, and it was in the South. I'd rented me a moving company, and the things I wasn't going to take, I left to Valeria, like most of the things in my son's room. The woman who'd wrecked my car turned out to be a Southern girl. Now it might seem that I'd chosen Georgia because of this coincidence, but that wouldn't be true. I did it to see a different light around me.

Theresa was a nurse and had a daughter that was six years old. When she told me she was a nurse, I thought she was kidding. Her beauty was a model's beauty, but it's true what people say: you see more, but there is something greater underneath it all. That was Theresa. A southern peach with class. When I told her I was moving to Georgia, she laughed. Her family was from Georgia, and she'd been living in New York for less than six years. She'd come up to study nursing. I used the car accident information to get to know her. We'd go out on a few dates and were comfortable with each other. I didn't want to create a scene. I told her I was married but separated, and she told me that her daughter's father was a sperm donor and nothing more. We continued to talk to each other up to the night I was leaving for Georgia. I gave her my house information and told her when she comes down to visit her family, stop in and see me. She said she would.

I'd found a real estate agent two weeks before I'd actually moved, and that was a good thing. I would drive down to Stormville, Georgia, to prepare my living condition. The house had five rooms and two bathrooms that were very spacious. It was better than the house I had in Queens and didn't cost as much with the mortgage. It was on one and an half acres of land surrounded by a beautiful view of trees that stretched as far as the eye could see. The first time I saw it, I knew that it was made for me. I walked through every room to get a feel of its ambiance, and it all felt good to me. That's why I bought the house. My son would enjoy its freedom and the country atmosphere.

It was a good change that I needed. New York City had become too stifling for me. People always asking for money or they're asking me to invest in their business. Talking about businesses, my Uncle Sandman called me a week before I was leaving New York. He wanted to know if I needed him to help me move. I told him that everything was fine. I asked him how were things going with the balloon flavors business. There was a brief pause on the line as I patiently waited for him to answer. When he did, I could tell by the tone of his voice that he was about to go through a long-winded explanation. I didn't want to go through it at the moment, so I gave my uncle an out. I told him that the money loss was okay, and that I knew he'd have his breakout moment when the time came. He thanked me, and I told him I loved him. My uncle was a man who had dreams, and he wanted to see those dreams come true before he became too old, and I respected that. He was a man who relied on his own wits and cunning. He was a good man looking to do great things.

As I settled into the climate of Atlanta, I would drive around, getting familiar with the town I was living in as well as the city itself. Atlanta, I would come to find out as the weeks ticked by, was a city of many cultural entities. I met people who'd I probably never meet in New York, and they were good people who enjoyed the South. I felt free to the point where I didn't have to feel like I had to have my guard up like whenever I met someone in New York. I was a celebrity who had money, and mostly those who knew that tried to manipulate me in some form or another. It's like I'd become a magnet for every person's dream to come true by investing in their ideas. I was going through a difficult time living in New York. Not anymore though. Atlanta gave me solace.

One morning after working out at the gym, I drove past a billboard that was advertising the opportunity to become a peace officer in Atlanta. It caught my attention. A peace officer? Why not. I wasn't working. I was writing my autobiography at the time and had writer's block that had me struggling for the right words. I needed something to get my thoughts going again. I'd been writing my life story for about three years, and at that moment, I had a total of twenty-eight pages. My mind needed a stimulant to refocus my thoughts and words. What was a peace officer? I asked myself as I continued to drive while looking at the billboard through my rearview mirror.

That night as I sat in front of my computer, I began researching what a peace officer was in Atlanta. The description was almost like a police officer. A person went to training, learned about the law, watched film on what was expected of him, as well as carrying a gun. I found this intriguing. Was I really attracted to this kind of environment after enduring what I suffered over the years while doing time? I would be on the opposite side of the fence, learning police procedures whereas half my life I had been incarcerated learning how to survive in prison. Could that be possible? Could I reverse my thinking and become what had once been thought of as an inhuman subculture because people in authority had taken their position and rammed it down the throats of those less fortunate and living in urban areas? Did I possess the mental makeup to live that way? To take on the role of being an enforcer of the law? I would really have to think it through. It was a leap into a pool of boiling hot water that could blister me for the rest of my life. I laughed at its ironic symbolism.

Three days later, I was still laughing as I began filling out the paperwork for becoming a peace officer. They asked me questions that ranged in the form of many things. There was the question of me ever being arrested that had me stumped for a minute. How do you answer that one? I asked myself. I'd been arrested and served a lot of time behind that arrest, but I'd also been exonerated and was told by the district attorney that my record was clean and that I could apply for any job I wanted. So do I put "yes" I was arrested but freed or do I put "no" because I had never been arrested with my record being cleared. There were other questions that took the reader into a complicated world, I thought, as I signed to have a drug test, urinalysis, blood test, physical, and to have an FBI do a background check of my life. I signed everything. After signing everything, I went home later that day and stared at my laptop for over an hour. The following hour, I began writing my autobiography again. Maybe I needed something different in my life to get me going. Whatever it was that sparked my mind to start writing, I made sure to get as much of it out as possible. I wrote for twenty hours.

Two weeks would go by after I'd completed the paperwork for peace officer. I was in the basement of my house installing a new flat-screen television when I saw I'd missed a call. It was a number I didn't recognize. I usually didn't answer unknown numbers, but for some reason, I was attracted to the call. It had a Georgia area code. I'd known only one person who had my number. That was Theresa. I called the number back several hours later.

I had learned to be suspicious of things after my release from prison. I didn't believe in coincidences. If something occurred, it did so with a purpose. I had to come to terms in my life that it would always be different, but I had to work it through with time, and that was something I had been considering while I'd lived in an eight by twelve cage for fourteen years. Some people might ask me why I'm not bitter or filled with hate because of how the law violated me, but I had no time to feel sorry for myself during those years of incarceration as I tried to get out. It made no sense to hate anyone. Why? That wouldn't have changed all the years I'd lost, and that energy could be directed to other positive things. No. I would never get caught up in the concept of hate. I learned that hating always came with a price. Sometimes, that price is too costly to a man's moral consciousness.

I'd arranged to meet Theresa at a restaurant a few miles from my house. I'd decided to wear a casual suit jacket, khaki pants, brown loafers, and a white shirt. I didn't want to stand out. I'd been thinking about Theresa for a minute. I thought she was a brainy woman who said what she meant when talking to her. She was a serious woman. Opposite of Valeria. She wanted to create her own clothing line in a few years. She'd been designing clothing ever since she was twenty years old. I like her enthusiasm and eagerness to make something of herself.

I'd arrived ten minutes early at the restaurant to make sure our table was right. The restaurant was fairly full with a multicultural atmosphere of patrons. I sat and sipped on some water. My wait for Theresa wasn't a long one. She was on time. I was mesmerized when she walked into the restaurant. She was wearing a two-piece burgundy dress suit with a black, silk blouse. Jet-black hair was pulled back to enhance her high cheekbones. Her face shone with small sparkles around her eyes. She was beautiful. I stood up as she neared the table.

"You're looking...beautiful," I said as I watched her smile and sit down.

"And you're looking handsome," Theresa said as she placed her small purse on the table. "What would you like to eat?"

I smiled. "I'm thinking about a steak, potatoes, corn on the cob. What about you?" I asked.

When she straightened her suit jacket, I caught a whiff of her perfume. It smelled flowery and fresh. I watched her gently touch the corner of her hair to smooth it out and was instantly attracted to her long, delicate fingers. I had to catch myself from staring at her beauty. Like any man who sees a beautiful woman, he savors that beauty like a toxic wine. You don't want to drink it too quickly but sip it with delicacy.

I had been cautious since my separation from Valeria. It was a caution that was done merely out of protecting my emotions rather than anything else. Sure, I knew that I should be aware of the fact that people might be trying to get close to me for my money. To play me in hopes that I'd fall prey to their game and manipulate me for whatever they think they could get from me.

"I'm thinking about salmon, a salad, and a glass of Chardonnay," Theresa said.

Even while listening to her voice, I felt a sense of calmness. The woman carried herself with aplomb. I found myself growing more and more attracted toward her as I sat in front of her listening to her. Yet I didn't want to get myself in a crushing situation that might embarrass me. I wanted to let Theresa take the lead, and if she wanted more, then I wanted her to initiate the bonding.

"I looked you up on the Internet, Anthony Faison," Theresa said as the waiter brought over our drinks. "Before getting involved with any man, I make sure I'm not placing my daughter in harm's way."

She knew about my past, and that's why she'd agreed to have dinner with me, I thought, as I sipped from my glass while glancing at her.

"First, I want to tell you that your experience is not a rarity in America's criminal judicial system. I have read stories of men like you in similar circumstances. Yet I'm sorry that you had to endure the loss of so many years that never took the time to correctly give you the benefit of doubt. Secondly, my seeking you out on the Internet was more of safety than anything else. I don't want you to feel offended. There are men out there who go to great lengths to impress women who are single parents by creating a facade that they are interested in them and then either steal their life savings or sexually abuse their child. Third and lastly, how do you give back to those who are less fortunate than you at the moment?"

My mouth fell open. My mouth felt like it was on the floor as I watched Theresa lift her glass to her mouth and drink demurely. Her words were powerful and real. I'd never met a woman who could form words that not only made you listen to what she had to say, but also appreciated the way she said it.

"Do you give speaking engagements about your experience?" Theresa asked.

"I did a few when I was in New York, but I haven't done anything since moving down here," I said as I stared at her.

"You should. Go to a few of the high schools and elementary schools down here. You might want to speak to a counselor who could assist you in getting in to talk to at-risk adolescents. Male and female. I think you can change a lot of people's lives if they could hear your life story. When I read about it on the Internet, I was surprised. You carry yourself like any other person, but inside, you're very special to do what you did, and I feel no animosity flowing from you."

"Maybe I will," I said, and when I said it, it was the truth. I wasn't lying to her to impress her. I was telling her something that I felt deep in my heart that should happen.

"What have you decided to do? I mean have you found a job yet? I know you don't think the money you were awarded will last forever. That will run out one day and then what?" Theresa asked as she placed her elbows on the table. "Please don't tell me you're one of those men who thinks spending money without earning money will make your life better."

"No. I—"

"Well, I'm impressed. God didn't get you out of prison to forfeit the gift he gave you," Theresa cut me off. "The world is a complicated pickle, and if you don't find yourself, then what is the purpose? And finding yourself means letting the world know what you've been through. If you constantly keep that story of yours in the open for the world to see, others wouldn't have to follow your experience who have been wrongfully convicted."

Theresa was right. She'd shown me a different light to enter into, and it was a light that had wonderful promises in it, I thought.

We ate dinner and talked about everything. She was bright. She could give as much as she received as far as being knowledgeable. She talked of things that I'd never dreamed a woman would think of. Politics. Family issues, as well as relationships. She mentioned the fact that men of color have a difficult time in having no commitment. I stopped her on that subject, and we laughed.

I went home that night and began writing in my book again. It was 2007, and I felt so alive after talking with Theresa. She was a woman that didn't rely on her looks. She had a brain and wasn't afraid to use it. As I stared at the blank page in front of me, I let my mind run free as I began to form paragraphs, sentences, and dialogue with each flick of my finger as they came alive with each stroke of the keyboard, and it felt good.

As the months went by, I continued to write my life story. I didn't want a book that talked negative; I wanted to create a piece of work where a person reading my book could be motivated in their lives to make it better no matter what their situation might be. Life can be very painful if an individual doesn't know what they want to do with their life. We can go into the military for the love of our country, we can join priesthood with the hopes that it will make a difference when a person comes to confession; there are those who feel that becoming a teacher to enlighten lives would benefit all those willing to be taught. Life is as complex as the stars above, but we keep opening our eyes every day, knowing in our hearts that one day our lives will get better. This concept is so true. If a person believes in what they are doing, that person's life has the chance to make a change in other's lives with positivity.

Theresa and her daughter, Brianna, moved in with me a year and a half after we'd met. I thought I'd never let another woman live with me after Valeria. I didn't want that connection nor did I want to feel concerned. Women have a tendency to want more from a man once they begin living with them. I'd experienced that with Valeria. Yet I couldn't lump Theresa in the same clay of one for all because she was different. She was a woman who marched at the sound of her own drum, and I respected her for that. She helped me with the bills as the months progressed. I didn't have to ask for money. Each time she got paid, she would bring me money and tell me to use it to pay the bills. A very strong woman.

By the end of 2009, I'd received in the mail a letter of acceptance regarding the peace officer position. I was dumbfounded at receiving the letter. If I complete my eight-week training course, I would be a peace officer. Unbelievable, I thought, as I'd sat on the edge of my bed, gingerly cradling the piece of paper. It could only happen in America. I'd once been deemed a criminal by a society that had used my peers to convict me of a crime I hadn't committed, and several years later, I was given the opportunity to walk on the other side of the fence of law. Breathtaking, I thought, as I smiled while reading the letter over and over.

When the time came for me to go into my eight-week training session for peace officer, I had purchased the recommended article clothing. Utility belt, black ankle-high boots, extra pants and shirts, and several other items. I received training in many areas of the street. My most thrilling encounter was learning how to shoot a firearm.

I'd never shot a gun before in my life. The average man may think that pointing a gun at another man is cool, but let me tell you, as I'd learned to properly hold a gun while firing it, the feeling you have isn't what you might see on television. It is a scary experience. Firing a gun like a Glock nine millimeter, M-16 rifle, and many other powerful firearms teaches you to respect a gun. I became less frightened of the weapons as I watched training films on how a person can kill me and what to do to stop them. I became a wonderful shot as the weeks worn on. I also took the lead in understanding a person's legal rights and appreciate human life that much more.

One day, it really hit me as I sat in class the last week of the eight-week course. I had once been incarcerated for fourteen years. I'd adapted to that environment to survive. Now, as I watched the instructor walk us through a defensive tactical film, reality really dawned on me. From a convicted felon, although exonerated, to a peace officer. Life had taken a turn of events in my life that might even seem untrue if I hadn't lived it. You might even say it could be written as a good screenplay if I hadn't actually lived through it all, I thought and smiled as I continued watching the film.

I believe, though, deep in my heart, that becoming a peace officer is what I'd wanted as a young man growing up in my urban setting. Why else could I pick through the legal jargon so easily while in prison or can see a situation and determine the legal outcome of it before it ever reached certain levels in my analytical mind? Certain things in life I could never really grasp quickly, but there were other things that I could envision immediately and see its outcome. Accepting my fate as a peace officer, I became interested in applying for other offices that were in conjunction with peace officer. I sought out the fugitive recovery officer, a private detective, as well as a US Marshall. I went crazy studying and training to become all the above and graduated in each training class.

After being approved by the state of Alabama, I began seeking out those who'd either failed to make their court appointments or were on the run from the law from other legal encounters. My first time going out on a bail-jumping job was an awesome experience. I, along with two other fugitive recovery officers, was in Wilbor, Tennessee. We'd been waiting for a man by the name of Thomas Shato. He was wanted for failure to appear in court on drug charges. Mr. Shato was also a well-known drug supplier for a Colombian drug cartel who was feared in Colombia. I thought that he'd fled back to his native homeland, but upon further investigation, we realized that his criminal history was that of a person who was quick to fire a weapon at law enforcement rather than give up. That was a surprise to me, especially since I didn't find out about it until the night of the stakeout.

Well, it was about three-thirty in the morning when Hodges, the lead and initiator of our trip, radioed that Shato had exited the building we'd been monitoring. Hodges had used one of his CIs to help us locate Shato when we first started out. Hodges had been doing fugitive work for over twelve years, and he used his knowledge of people to work his way in the direction that led us to where we were sitting at that moment. The apartment was a girlfriend's place. It was located in a dark, ghetto area. Some of the men I watched while waiting appeared to be ruthless and cunning as they passed our vehicle. There were a few times when I reached for my weapon as my eyes locked with a shady character walking by the car. This was new to me. The stakeout as well as the tension I felt while keeping my eyes constantly moving for anything out of the ordinary. Hodges informed us that Shato was walking away from our location and around the opposite direction. I glanced at Chaz who was sitting beside me. He too was an experienced fugitive officer. He nodded for us to get out of the car after radioing the information.

When I exited the car from the passenger side, I looked around as I hefted my bulletproof vest that I was wearing to make sure it was secure. I readjusted my holster that held my Glock seventeen-shot weapon. My shoes, a pair of black Tech boots, were tied tightly at the ankles. I looked at Chaz. He tossed his head in the direction that we were to go. As I walked around the hood of the gray Impala that we were driving, the radio in Chaz's hand crackled with Hodges's urgent voice telling us that Shato had spotted him and was on the run. Chaz and I, with no time to think, took off running in the direction that Hodges had been sitting in another car around the corner.

As Chaz and I turned the corner, fifteen or twenty seconds later, I could see Hodges sprinting down the street away from us. Without thinking, I took off running in pursuit of Hodges and our fugitive, Shato. With my left hand holding a flashlight and my right hand occasionally falling onto my holstered weapon, I increased my speed to catch up. Chaz was behind me, but after ten minutes of running, I could hear his labored breathing. He was over one hundred and ninety pounds. I knew as long as he was behind me, no one could outflank us, so I ran faster.

My hesitation and fear of the unknown had dissipated as I continued to run. Hodges was a good man. He'd asked me to come for the experience. I wouldn't feel right if I'd let him down and something happened to him. I ran faster, and as I did, the sound of gunfire momentarily stopped me in my tracks. I shook that off within seconds and then took off in the direction in which I'd heard the shot. It'd come from a building up ahead. It was the same area in which I'd seen Hodges disappeared. I glanced behind me to see Chaz doubled over, trying to catch his breath. He waved for me to go ahead. I didn't look back a second time as I ran toward the back of the building.

When I turned the corner, flashlight still in hand, I was greeted with the sound of more gunfire and the wheezing of something passing my left ear made me fall to the ground and rolled to the left of me while turning off my flashlight. It was instinctive. My training had kicked in like a second skin. I saw Hodges hiding behind a car a few feet away. He nodded when our eyes met. I pulled my weapon and waited for Hodges to tell me what to do. My hand was sweating as I gripped my weapon. I felt perspiration running down my face and my back. My breathing was difficult and irregular as I tried to concentrate and gather my thoughts. With the pounding of footsteps behind me, I shouted to Chaz to turn off his flashlight and come in with caution. No one knew where Shato was concealed. It was dark with no moonlight. He could be hiding anywhere. He had the advantage.

I heard Hodges shouting to Shato to give himself up or he'd be in worse trouble when caught for shooting at bail recovery agents. There was silence. Hodges continued by asking if Shato wanted to get his girlfriend in trouble. Still, the silence continued. I looked at Chaz. He shrugged. His expression was lackadaisical. Was I really hiding behind a car with my weapon in my hand, contemplating firing it? I wiped the perspiration out of my eyes with my forearm. If I were there, then I was there for a reason, and if I had to, I would protect myself as well as Hodges and Chaz. If it meant taking a man's life to ensure that, then that's what I'd do in hopes of seeing the rise of another sunset and seeing the face of my daughter, Imanee. Theresa had given me a child. A beautiful child who looked exactly like me, and at that moment, with death looming, I realized that I loved Theresa. I mean, heart-pounding love. Sometimes, we let things slip by us because we figure those things will always be there, but when we see them slipping away, we want to grab hold of them and keep them close to our heart. All my efforts at that instant would be to guarantee that I survive. I'd survive fourteen years in prison. I'd be damned if I'd done all that to die in an alley.

I heard Hodges call out again to Shato. Asking him to give up. That if we came for him, things would be very messy. I heard a grunt come from the right of me. Small, but it was there. I was about to stick my head up when I felt Chaz grab my arm. I looked at him quizzically. He shook his head. He indicated that I should keep my head down and out of sight.

Hodges called out again, and by the tone of his voice, I knew the situation was about to get very ugly as he gave Shato on the count of ten to come out peacefully or we were coming in to get him with our guns blazing. I listened as the countdown began.

One.
I licked my dry lips.

Two.
My throat became tight as I blinked out the perspiration from my eyes.

Three.
I looked at Chaz. He gave me a reassuring nod and a weak smile.

Four.
I felt the muscles in my arms tighten as I prepared to spring up and begin firing my weapon.

Five.
I exhaled nervously.

Six.
I began shaking my head. We are going in to get him. It would be a do or die situation.

Seven.

There comes a time when prayer could be so invigorating, but at that moment, I wasn't thinking about praying. It was the farthest thing from my mind.

Eight.

I flicked off the safety switch on my weapon. It had come down to this. Man to man and whoever's aim was better, then the other person was dying in the street tonight.

Nine.

I rearranged my position to leap up when the time was right. I took in deep breaths as I gathered my wits about me. All the training I'd received was heightened. I was wound like a wristwatch. I was ready to pounce.

The sound of metal hitting the ground caught my ears. Following that, I heard Shato say he was coming out unarmed. I glanced at Chaz. He was smiling. Seconds later, I watched Hodges slowly rise. Keeping his head out of full view in case Shato had another weapon. With caution, Chaz and I both began to rise as well.

I saw Shato walk out from behind a large metal trash container. His hands were up, but I continued to keep my Glock nine millimeter pointed at the center of his chest. The largest cavity to aim at when firing. He walked out into the open. Hodges approached him with his gun pointed at him. I heard Hodges tell him to turn around and put his hands on the metal trash container. He complied. I came out from behind the car and walked toward Shato. My senses were doubly heightened as I approached him. Chaz was to the right of me with his weapon aimed at Shato. If the man made the slightest move, he would be shot, I thought. Hodges placed the handcuffs on him with no incident, and only then, did I sigh with relief.

On our way back to Atlanta, I was driving with Hodges. Shato was in the backseat sleeping. I was exhausted as I listened to Hodges say where I'd made my mistakes. My adrenaline was fading, but I made sure to digest all that he was informing me what not to do next time. I said nothing as I took everything in earnestly. He was teaching me, and I was eager to learn the profession.

With the experience of fugitive recovery, I also began doing part-time work as security in nightclubs. It gave me the chance to network and talk to owners of these clubs while making two hundred dollars a night for four hours of work, five days a week. What I didn't know or wouldn't admit was that I was going into my own line of work as a private investigator. I'd go on a few other runs with Chaz and Hodges as the months went by. I needed to get under the paws of fugitives to see them react. To learn from their cornered, animalistic thought pattern. With Hodges, he taught me patience and cunning to anticipate their moves. And to this day, he and I are still the best of friends.

When 2010 rolled in, I was working at a Homeland Security building in Atlanta. Others might think that working there would be beneath me. That's the farthest from the truth. I enjoy my job as a peace officer. It takes me full circle out of a world of darkness that I'd spent fourteen years in and into a world of light that has shown me warmth as well as growth. I could never sit home and let bitterness take hold of me. Why? Would it change lost years in prison? No, it wouldn't. I had to change my thought pattern, and in doing so, I began to grow and my public service commitment became routine.

Becoming a contracted federal protective security officer allowed me the experience and interaction with the operations of the federal government. I learned quickly that politics rules all in federal buildings, individual rights came second. When I initially applied for the job and learned that I had to pass a federal background check and a federal adjudication I became concerned. Why should I worry? I passed every background check prior to this; however, the government wants to know who your high school teacher was. Would they find out about my past and then conclude that even though I was exonerated, that I am not worthy of such a security-sensitive position. A job that would require me to become the first line of defense for federal buildings that houses the Secret Service, ATF, Treasury Agents, US Marshals, and the FBI. To prevent the entry of explosives and contraband that could be detrimental to the security of every single occupant in that building. Those concerns would become harmless when I was cleared and given a post in that federal building several weeks later.

Now as I sit here reflecting on my journey through the criminal justice system so many years ago, and my journey of being free from the restraints of shackles that were once snapped securely on my wrists and ankles, I sleep with no regrets and no anger. I have a role to play in this world that we call life. By moving to the wonderful State of Georgia, it has given me the opportunity to become the first person in American history to accomplish what I am at the present. Although it has been a real, bumpy ride, it was a ride that has me now letting you read and experience what I went through, and if you can take anything from this story, make sure you take the concept that all things in life are not totally final. There's always a door open; you have to simply turn the knob and walk through it.